Fundamentals of Graphic Language
Practice Book

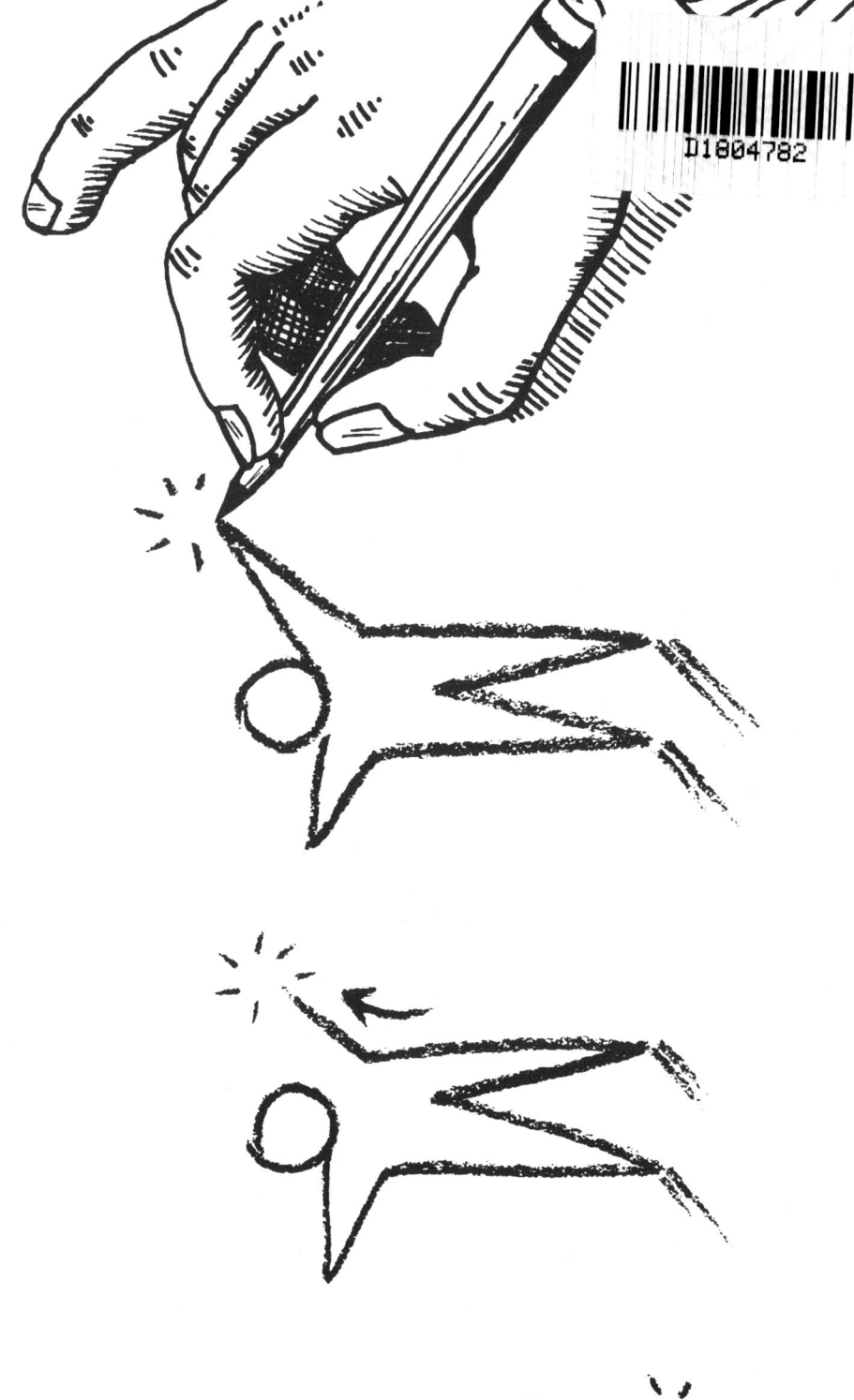

ISBN # 1-879502-00-3

©1993 The Grove Consultants International. Version 2.0 All rights reserved. No part of this book may be used or reproduced in any manner other than hand-done drawings without written permission except in the case of brief quotations embodied in critical articles and reviews.

For information address The Grove Consultants Int., PO Box 29391, San Francisco, CA 94129 USA.

Phone: 800/49GROVE or 415/561-2500

Fax: 415/561-2525

Web: www.grove.com

CONTENTS

CHAPTER 1	What is Graphic Language?	1
CHAPTER 2	How to Use This Book	7
CHAPTER 3	Your Body Knows!	11
CHAPTER 4	Lettering	37
CHAPTER 5	Seed Shapes	55
CHAPTER 6	Star People	109
CHAPTER 7	Putting It All Together	131

CHAPTER 1

What is Graphic Language?

RAPHIC LANGUAGE IS WHAT YOU USE WHEN YOU GESTURE, MOVE THINGS AROUND ON THE RESTAURANT TABLE TO MAKE A POINT, OR SKETCH IDEAS. Teachers, trainers, facilitators, consultants, inventors, designers, coaches, engineers, and anyone who wants to think about how organizations and systems work use graphic language as an integral part of their work.

It's our natural language

It's as natural as talking. You learned your first "visual words" from your mother's expressions and gestures before you learned her language. If you've played Pictionary, explored the Macintosh graphic computer, or been fascinated with Nintendo, you know how compelling graphic language can be. It's no surprise that businesses are buying copyboards, desktop-publishing hardware and software, and

1

all kinds of visual media for the same reasons. If you think about it, educators and trainers probably would give up every other tool except their blackboards and chart stands.

Graphics help groups see what they mean

I began using graphics for communication 20 years ago when I led seminars on public affairs for the Coro Foundation. The program involved groups of young people in exploring how cities work through internships with city leaders. The "fellows" would intern Monday through Thursday and meet Fridays to exchange insights and information. When we started drawing our ideas on the wall in addition to talking, the seminars came alive and we were able to work very powerfully as a group. The simplest drawings worked best. We would literally see what we meant.

Drawing leads to insights

These successes led me to spend five years exploring everything that could be done with people and blank paper by using graphics as an interactive language. I found that people get much more involved in visuals that are being drawn live than ones that are prepared in advance. I found that in visual dialogue, people can construct new meanings and often leap to new insights as wonderful "accidents" happen. I found that drawing is a way to train the brain to see and that group drawing helps groups to see. A new world of possibilities opened up.

Developing and teaching graphic language

I began exploring how to teach graphic language soon after I began using it. I looked at all the graphic languages used around the world and in ancient times. I found that the little pictures which are ideograms in China and Japan were created to allow countries to communicate and trade even though they spoke different languages. Over the years the original pictures have been simplified so much that they are almost in code, but they started the same way the drawings in this book started.

I found that there are many shapes that are the same around the world. So I set out to identify the most useful, common ones to provide a basic graphic "alphabet." These seed shapes turned out to have much in common with the basic strokes and gestures from which all drawings are created. I began to understand that all humans on Earth have roughly the same body structure and that the motions of the arm holding a stick or pen are very similar. Are the feelings associated with the drawing process responsible for the meaning of these shapes? I began to notice that people's natural arm gestures looked very much like fundamental strokes, if I just imagined them holding a pen while communicating.

Our bodies know how to draw

Then I discovered that if I could focus people's minds on simple images, their bodies would already know how to draw. Making the gestures had more to do with simply choosing a result and staying focused, than it did with a complicated activity. So I had people play around by making very large drawings on the wall. This kinesthetic experience was so powerful, and the excitement of everyone able to draw all the basic strokes was so thrilling, that people's drawings improved immediately.

I discovered that the same techniques used for big drawings applied to drawing while seated and working in a journal or notebook. The workshops began integrating the two, and I saw that as people found graphic language useful for themselves and used it in note-taking and personal creative work, their ability to use it on flip charts and large displays also increased. Apparently, the brain can scale up and scale down without much effort.

The biggest block turned out to be people's second and third grade decisions that they

couldn't draw. Some people had not tried since then and avoided all attempts. When they finally had direct experience of how easy it was, they were faced with a tough choice. Would they really be able to remake a decision they made clear back in the second grade, and admit they were wrong? Maybe it's more important to be right than have fun. Maybe people like to be consumers more than they like to be creators. But many people jumped right in and haven't looked back; using graphic language as a key part of everything they do—just like talking.

Graphics work cross-culturally

A whole network of people is now involved, using graphic language as a key tool in organizational development and communication consulting, and helping to literally "draw out the best in people." We work all over the world with every kind of organization you can imagine. We work with deaf people, disabled people, philanthropists, manufacturing teams, architects, politicians, bankers, gardeners. And graphic language works everywhere. There is no question that we've stumbled on one of the most natural and amazing tools we have as humans.

Reclaim your graphic birthright

This book shares the discoveries through which you, too, can reclaim this powerful and fun way to communicate. Drawing is magic any way you do it. It simply requires starting with the fundamental gestures and strokes out of which all simple drawings are created. The drawing guides your vision of these shapes and the vision helps the drawing. You'll begin to see the points, lines, angles and squares in everything. You will then combine the basic gestures into some "seed" shapes, which are little sequences for drawing people, blocks, arrows, and other building-block graphics. Next, you will learn how to invent new graphics and "grow" these seed shapes into more elaborate pictures. All of the drawings are the simple ones you will need to use graphics as an active language.

This book is called the *Fundamentals* because you'll have fun right from the start. By the end of this practice book, you will be able to draw every basic stroke and shape used to create almost all the graphics you will ever need to express yourself, or draw out what others are saying. Mastery comes with practice, of course, and grows with the invention and aliveness that is at the heart of any living language. Once your capability is unlocked, you'll find you have a virtually unlimited warehouse of graphic imagery from living in one of the most visually stimulating times in human history.

Have FUN!

DAVID SIBBET

David Sibbet

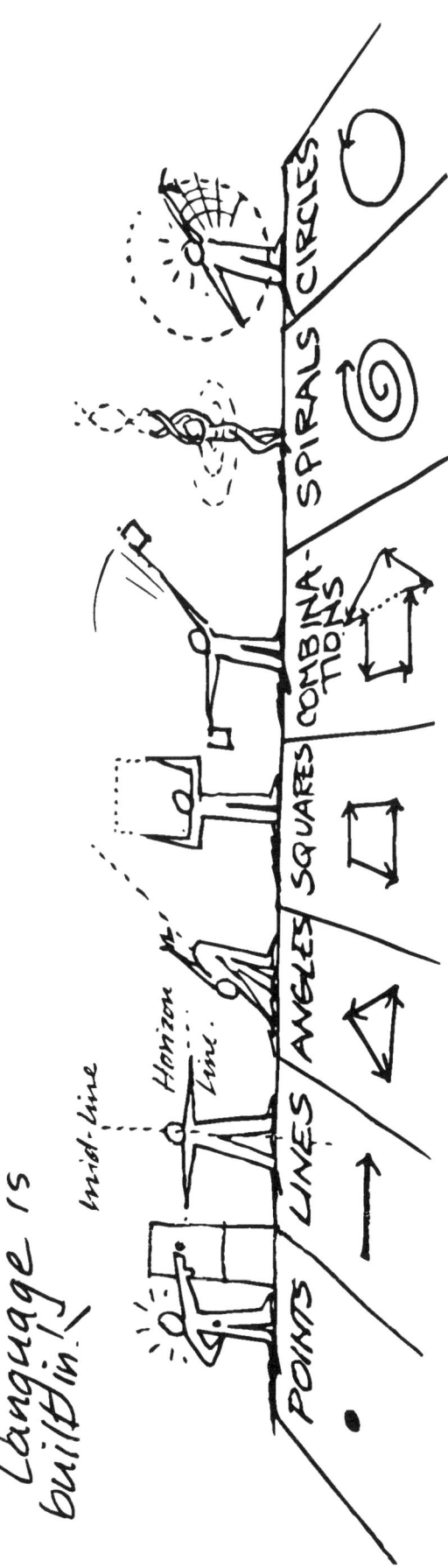

CHAPTER 2

How to Use This Book

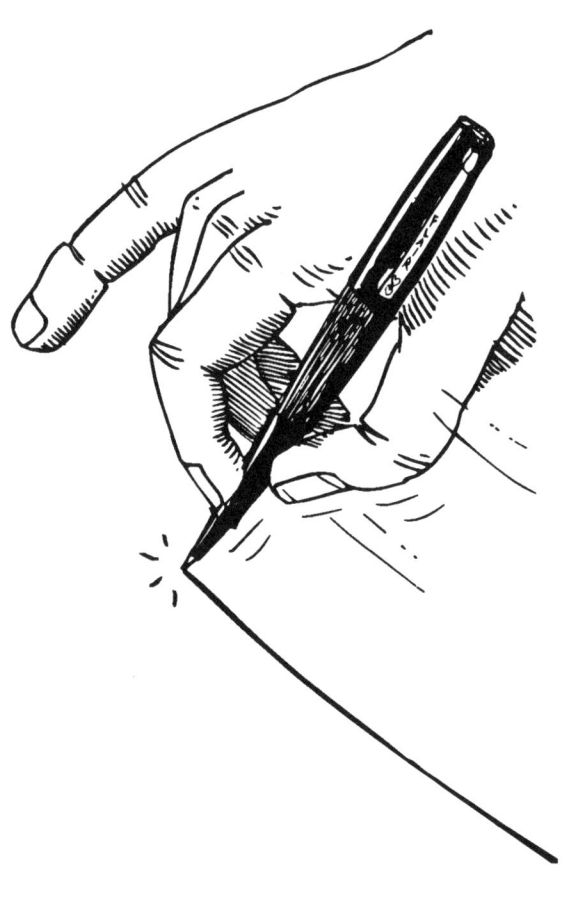

THIS PRACTICE BOOK INTRODUCES YOU TO THE FUNDAMENTALS OF GRAPHIC LANGUAGE. It moves step-by-step from basic strokes to basic letters to seed shapes, and then to improvisations which build on these fundamentals. Each chapter presents examples to follow and includes room to practice. All you need is a felt-tip pen and about an hour or so to get started. When you feel "full," take a break and let the work you've done soak in. Work through the book at your own pace using as many sessions as you need. If you already use graphics, find your own way of using the chapters as resources. And have fun!

Basic Practice

The drawing practices presented in this book begin with *centering your body, focusing your mind,* and *drawing!* These steps are introduced below and reviewed again in "Chapter Three: Your Body Knows!"

CENTERING involves sitting in a chair with both feet flat on the floor, both buttocks flat on the seat, and both of your arms lightly touching the desk top. When centered, it feels almost as though you are "perching" over the table like a bird about to fly. You might also feel like a tree, planted and straight, but flexible in the wind. Center by getting the pressure equal on both feet and both buttocks, and then imagining a golden line from the top of your head through your spine to the center on the earth. After a few times it becomes automatic. Centering also means getting a good hold on your pen, orienting your paper as suggested with each practice, and getting your whole body ready to draw.

FOCUSING involves your mind—your attention. In this practice book each exercise asks you to focus on a single image just before you draw. The focus you hold will trigger the drawing. If you find your drawings are a bit awkward, see if you can remember what you were focusing on. Was your mind completely concentrated on the suggested image, or were you holding other things in mind? Explore the connection.

DRAWING requires acting from focus, and accepting whatever the result is. Drawing feels like something between an arrow being released and a bird flying. Your mind is focused. Your body does the drawing. Drawing basic shapes must be centered in your body for best results.

CENTER

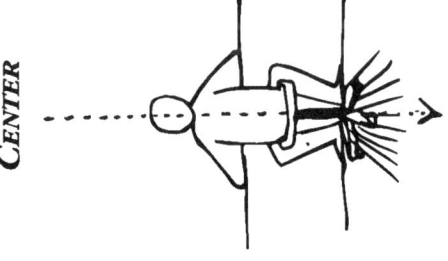

FOCUS

DRAW!

yea!

Accept

For basic practice, it is essential to accept whatever happens. The principle obstacle to reclaiming your drawing ability is your critical, judgmental mind that makes negative comments while you are working, which have nothing to do with your body's basic ability. The type of graphic language that works in creative sessions with yourself or colleagues, and in meetings, is actually very simple.

So accept whatever your body produces as the *key* to learning how it works with graphics. Think of your body as a fabulous bio-computer with amazing graphic programs built in. All you need to do to find its abilities is focus on various images, unleash the body, and notice the results.

Learning to accept and notice the things that do *not* fit your expectations is as important as accepting what does. A nice, curved line produced while you "think" you are doing a straight line is like a little puzzle. You were paying attention to something. What was it? Your body was centered in some way in the chair and in relation to the paper. How were you centered? Accepting any and all results and simply noting your center and focus will help you learn quickly.

If you find yourself being critical, accept that too! Notice what result it produces in your drawings.

Practice! Practice! Practice!

Repetition and practice are the best ways to discover what your body knows at the basic level. On this foundation you can add details and inventions. At a certain point, like kids and spoken language, it just takes off and flourishes.

CHAPTER 3

Your Body Knows!

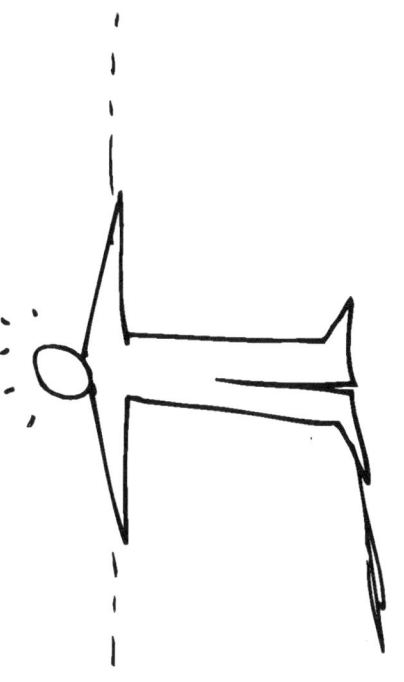

THIS CHAPTER TAKES DRAWING BACK TO ITS SOURCE—THE HUMAN BODY. The basic strokes used in drawing are natural to our human form—and that is why so much of the world's art contains similar shapes. Once you know the natural movements that generate these strokes, you can begin to use graphic language the way you use spoken language. The main challenge is convincing your head to let your body do the drawing!

The practices in this chapter begin with these basic strokes:

- The **drop line** which simply follows the line of gravity.
- The **horizon line** which follows the horizon.
- The **circle** which results when your arm compasses around your shoulder.

CENTER your body

It is important to prepare your body to do what it knows. This process is called "centering," as discussed in chapter two. It means to literally get your arms, torso, and legs balanced around your center of gravity. After you feel centered, imagine yourself looking down from the ceiling. Could you see right through your spine into the center of the earth, if your spine were a tube? Is the right edge of your paper lined up with your forearm, when it's resting lightly on the table?

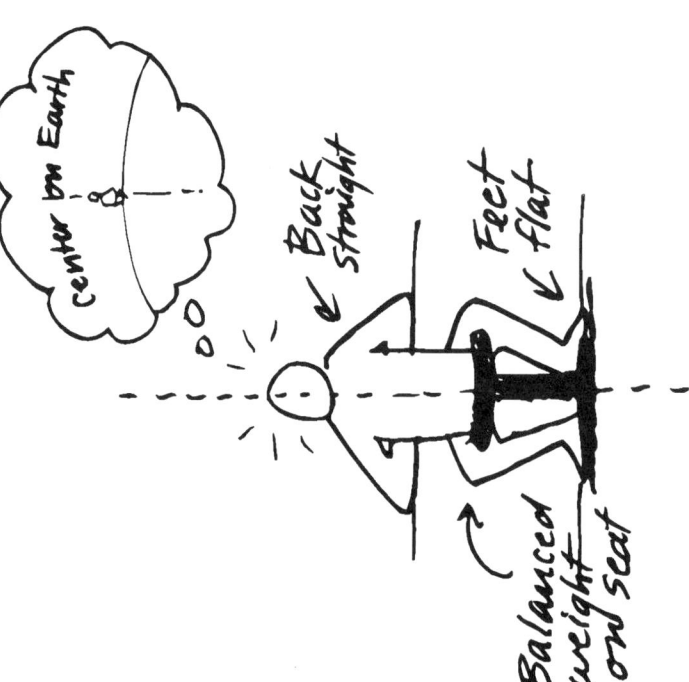

FOCUS your attention

As you learn these basic strokes your conscious mind needs to direct your attention to the desired result—in the case of horizontal and vertical lines your attention should be on the end point of the line, or with the curved lines on the "shape" you want. Once your mind is focused, the body follows automatically.

©1993 Graphic Guides Inc.

LEFT HANDED — Line up left arm & paper

RIGHT HANDED — paper directly in front...; arm; angles

DRAW! When you are centered and focused on the suggested image, DRAW! It is important to *experience* yourself drawing these strokes naturally. The best way is repeating the processes over and over—center, focus, draw. Accept results. Center, focus, draw. Accept results. Center, focus, draw. Accept results. Notice patterns. Center, focus, draw. It's that easy.

Point

- Focus on the cross points in the grid and rapidly draw a point. This is a kind of target practice for aiming your attention and letting your body follow.

The point means focus. Starting point, point of view, belly button.

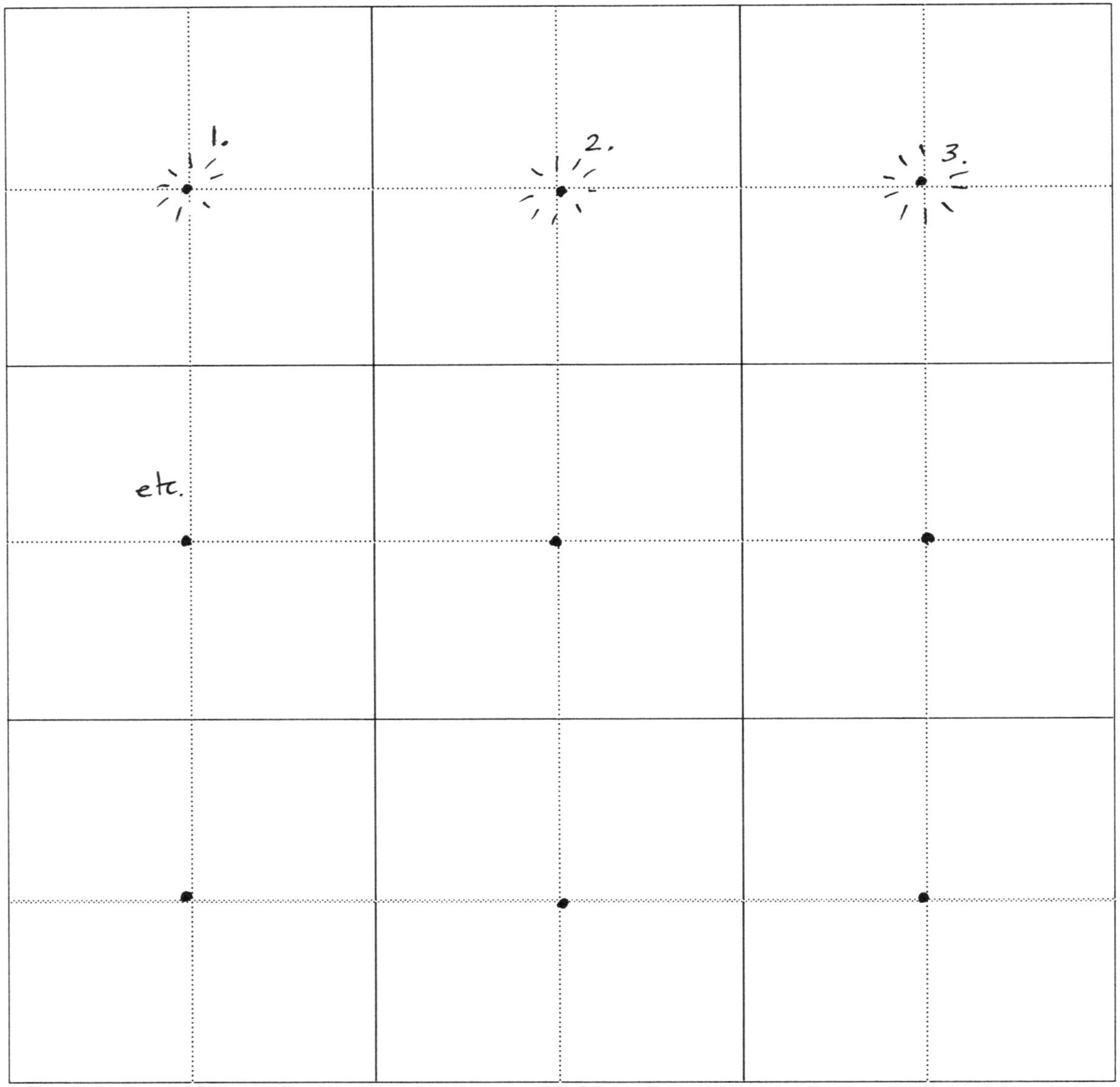

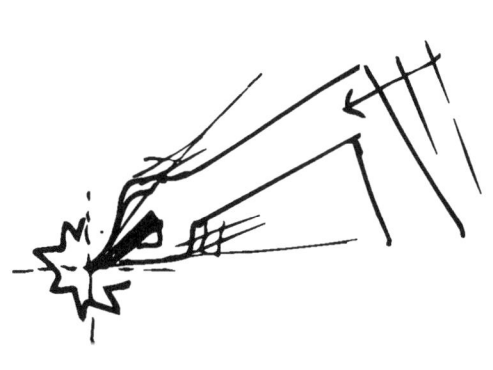

TIP *Shoot for the cross-hairs!*

Drop Lines

CENTER
- Sit with your feet on the floor, balance your weight on the seat.
- Align paper so the vertical edge is parallel with your forearm.
- Point your pen at the top of the line you are about to draw.

FOCUS
- Imagine your pen as a HEAVY ROCK that wants to drop to the bottom of the page.

DRAW
- "Drop" the line.

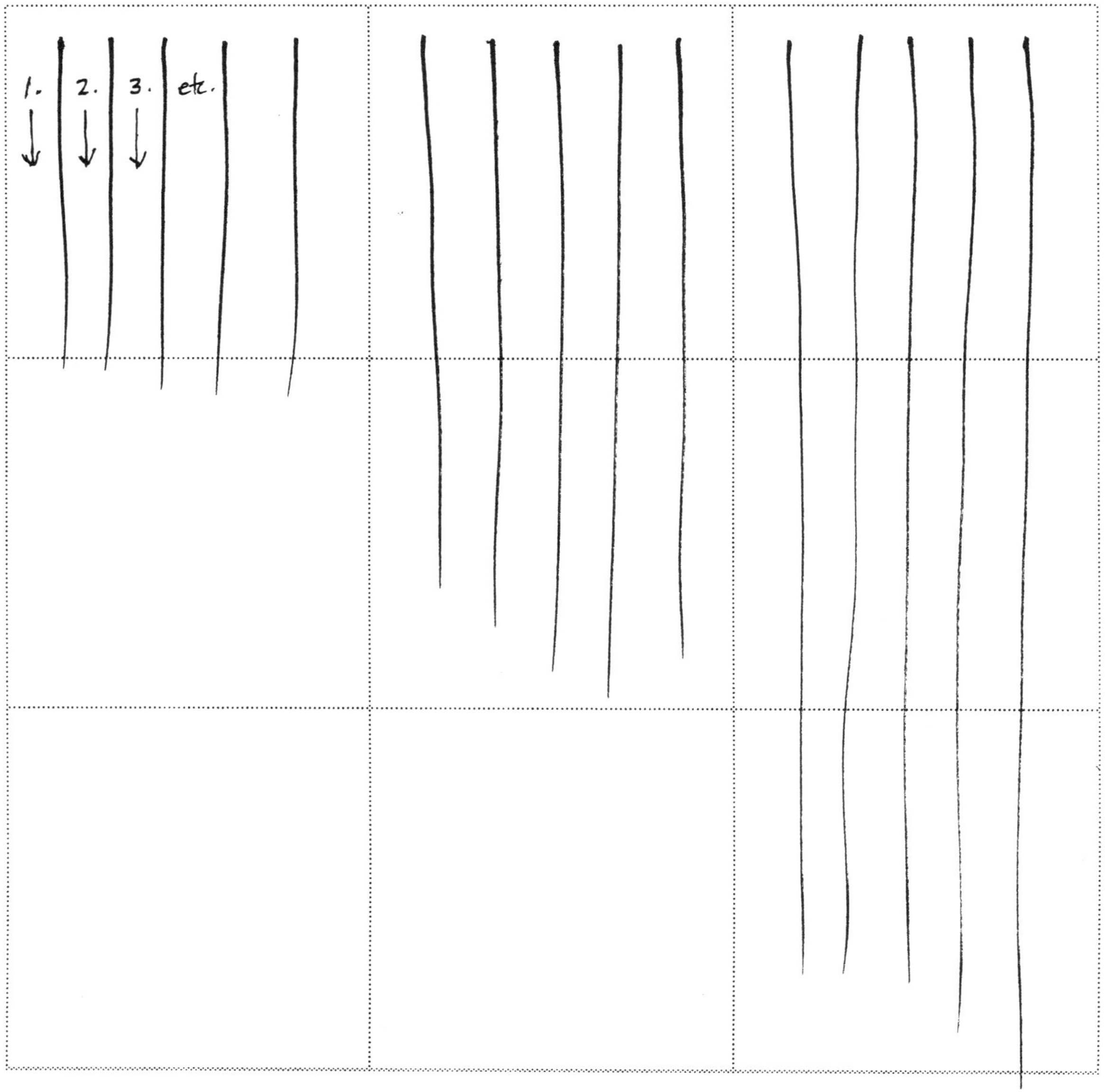

"Drop" the line down the page.

Page edge and forearm should be parallel

Horizontal Lines

CENTER
- Balance yourself over your paper.
- Align paper so the vertical edge is parallel with your forearm.
- Stiffen your wrist.
- Point pen to the start of the line.

FOCUS
- Imagine the LONG HORIZON where the sky meets the earth.

DRAW
- Draw a tiny piece of it.

wrist is locked

90°

draw pivoting from elbow

TIP Accept whatever happens.
Re-focus each time.
Simply notice what you are doing with each line.

— Are you centered?
— Are you focused?

Practice a few with your eyes closed.

Throw Lines

CENTER
- Balance yourself.
- Align the paper's vertical edge with your forearm.
- Point your pen at the start of the line.

FOCUS
- *Look at the* DESTINATION POINT.

DRAW
- Throw a line to the destination without looking at your pen.

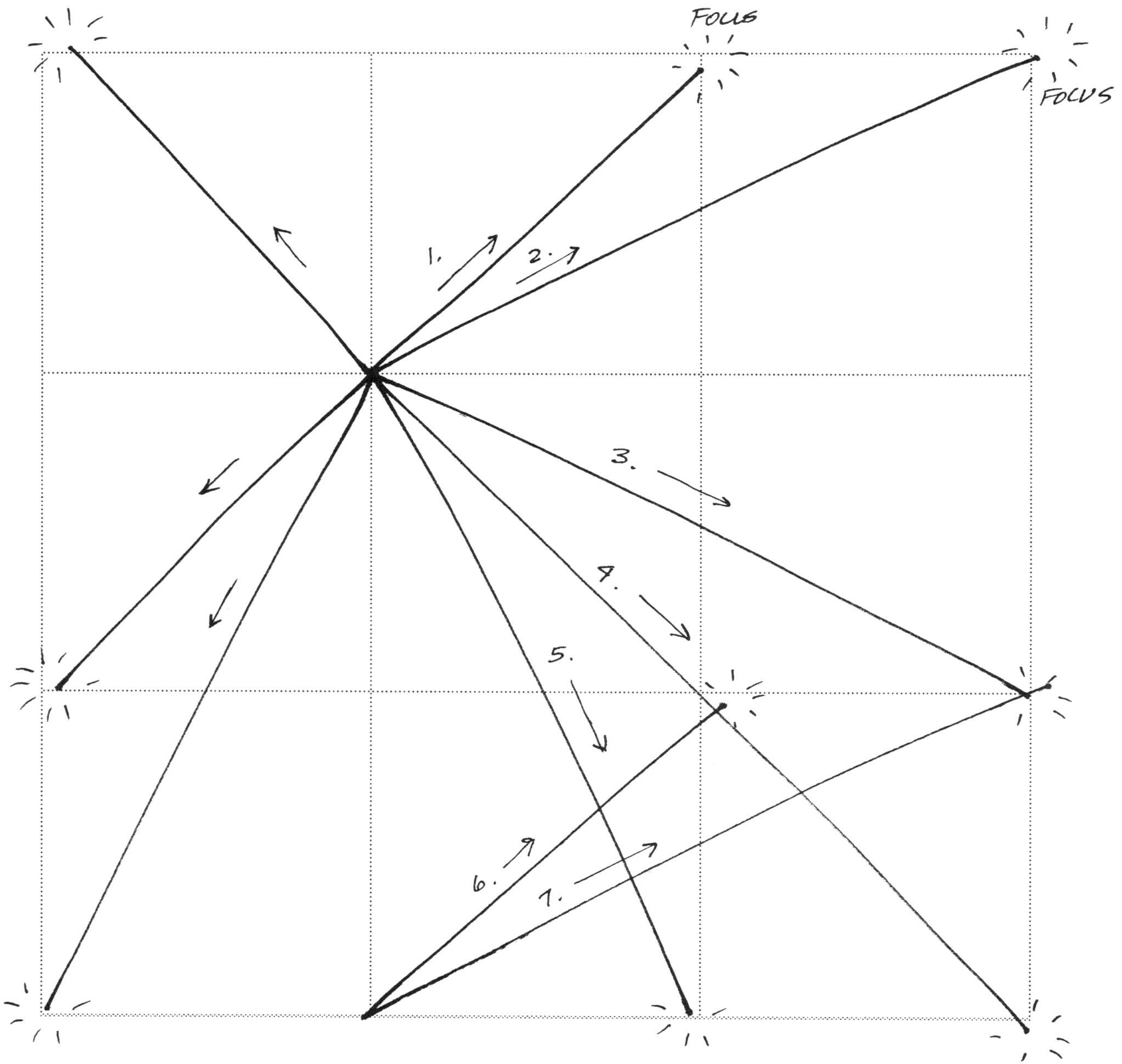

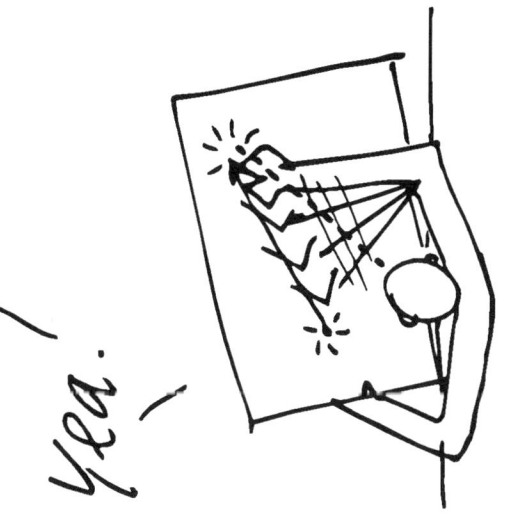

TIP *Centering means being only here, and completely open.*

Diagonal Lines

CENTER
- Balance yourself.
- Align paper with your forearm.
- Place pen at the start of the line.
  Lightly lock your wrist.

FOCUS
- **Concentrate on the DESTINATION POINT.**

DRAW
- Throw the line!

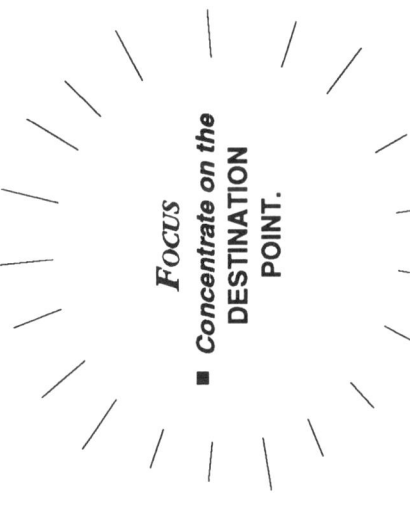

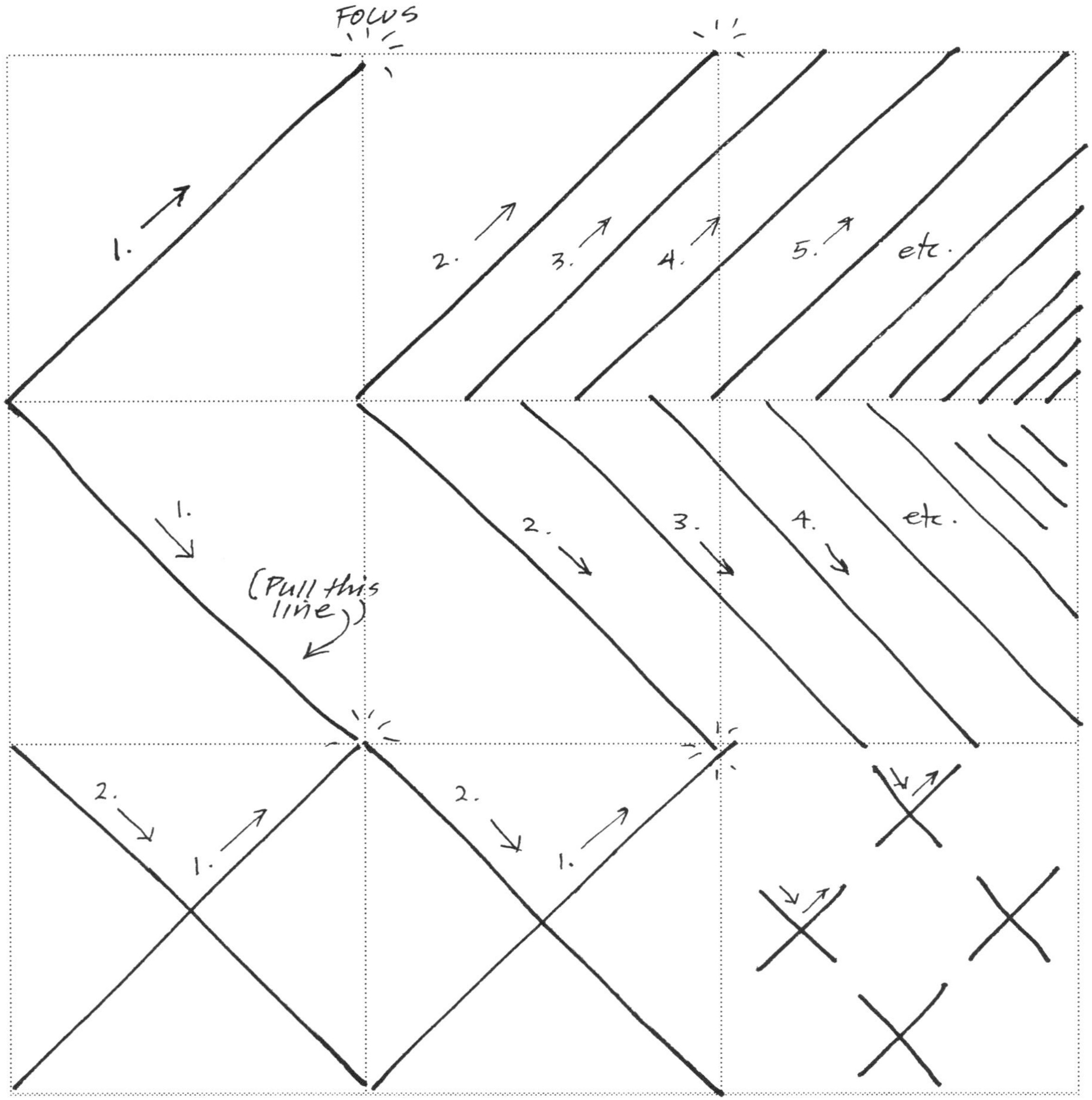

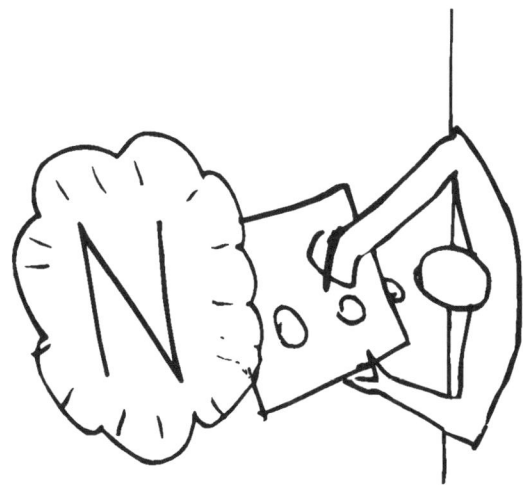

TIP *The line creates relationship. It separates, connects and shows the direction in which your drawing travels.*

Shading Lines

Draw shapes using the strokes you've already practiced in column 1. Draw a second shape offset from the first one in column 2.

CENTER

- Balance.
- Align the paper so shading lines will be perpendicular to your forearm.
- Lock your wrist.
- Hold your body as a frame for your rocking arm on the edge of the second shape.

FOCUS

- Watch the line which will throw the shadow as the starting point for each SHADING LINE.

DRAW

- Throw repeating diagonals, pivoting from your elbow.

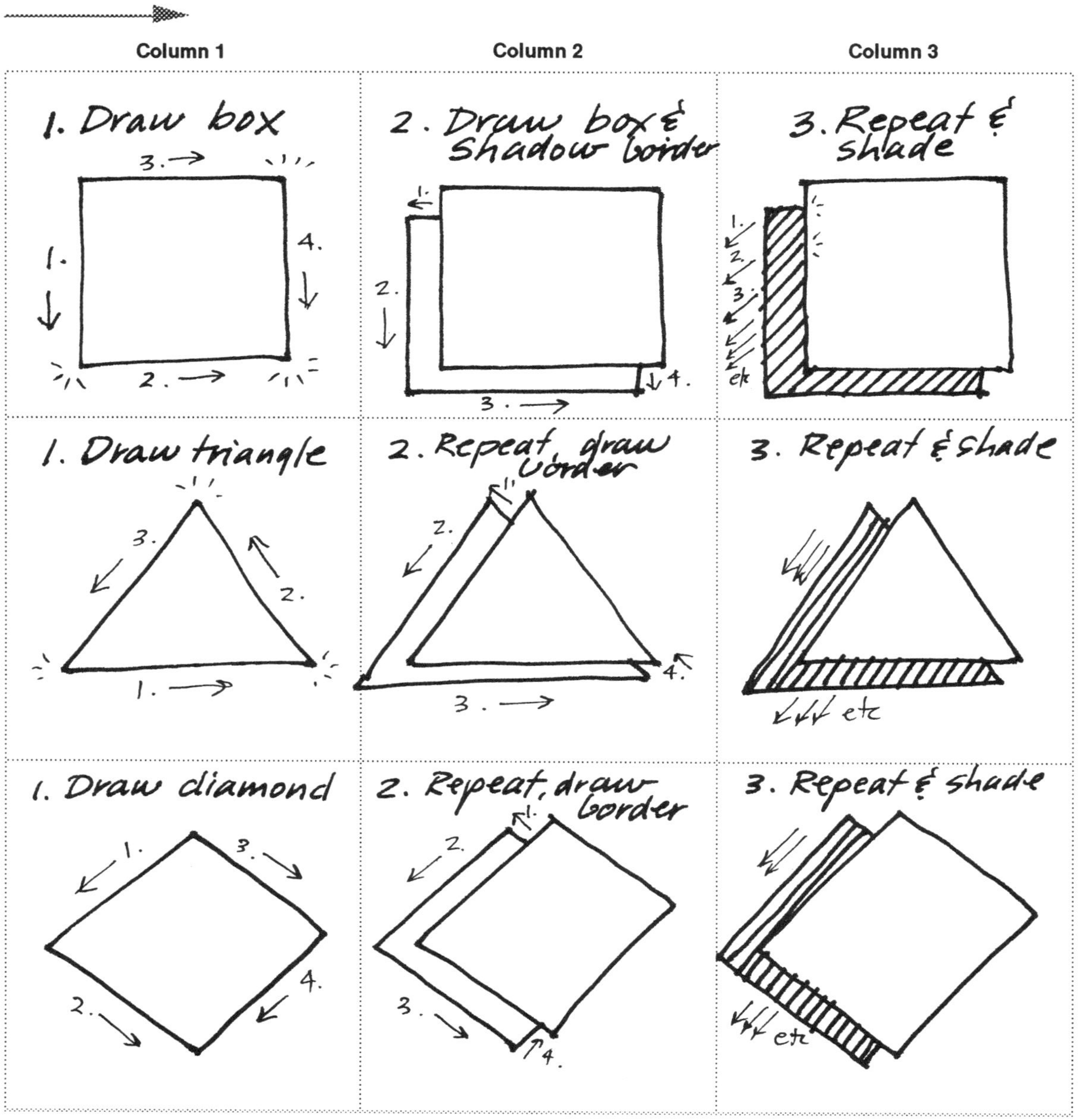

Column 1	Column 2	Column 3
1. Draw box	2. Draw box & shadow border	3. Repeat & shade
1. Draw triangle	2. Repeat, draw border	3. Repeat & shade
1. Draw diamond	2. Repeat, draw border	3. Repeat & shade

© 1993 Graphic Guides Inc.

Column 1	Column 2	Column 3

Hold wrist locked.

Lock arm from elbow.

Hold body as frame.

TIP *Shade to increase the feeling of volume and form.*

25 *Your Body Knows!*

©1993 Graphic Guides Inc.

Circles

CENTER
- Sit with your body balanced, both feet on floor.
- Perch over the paper—like you are flying.
- Lock your wrist and elbow, and let your arm hang from your shoulder like a pendulum.

FOCUS
- *Let your body FEEL the circular stirring motion. Move in a circle to focus the body.*

DRAW
- Touch pen to paper.

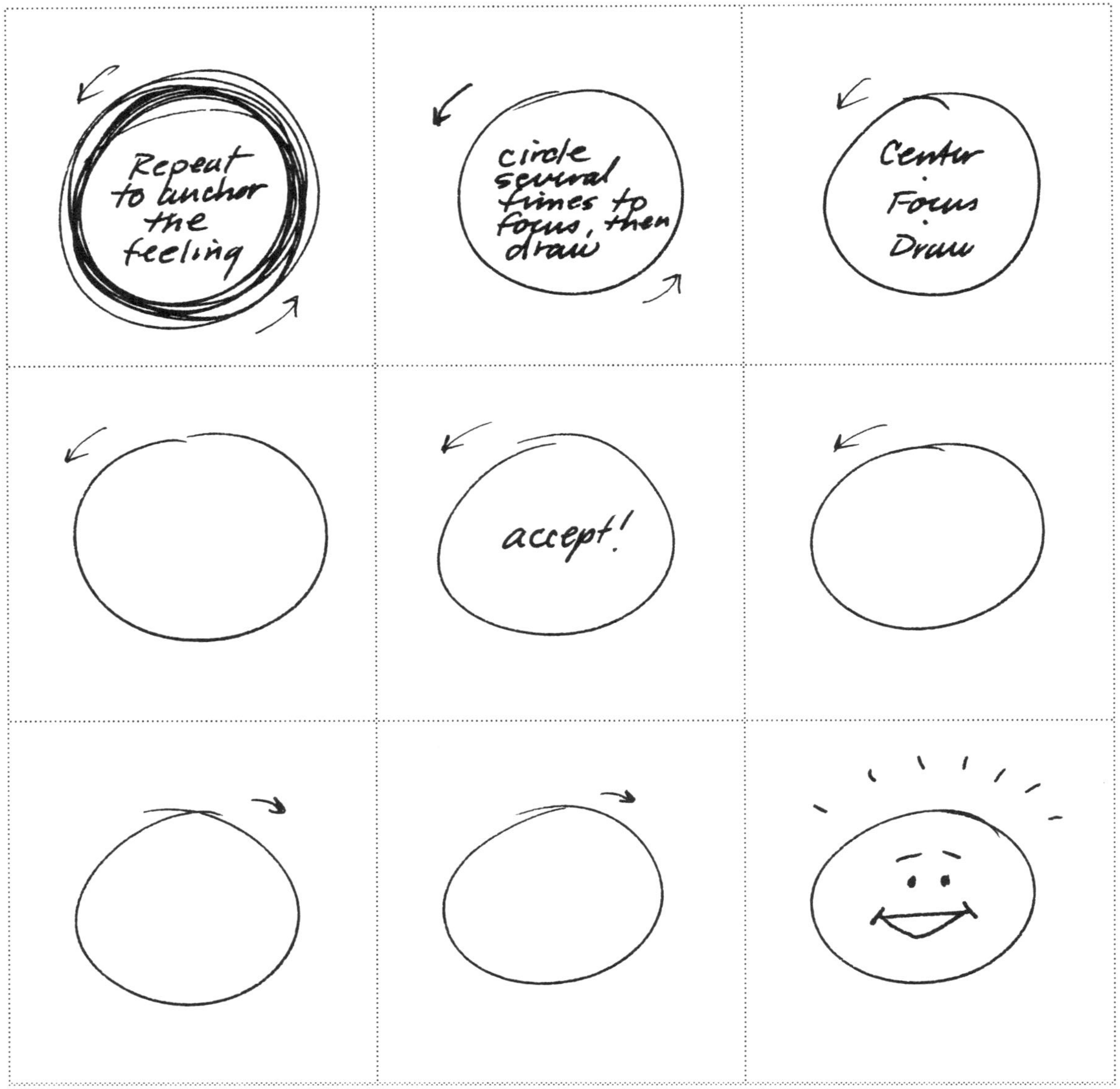

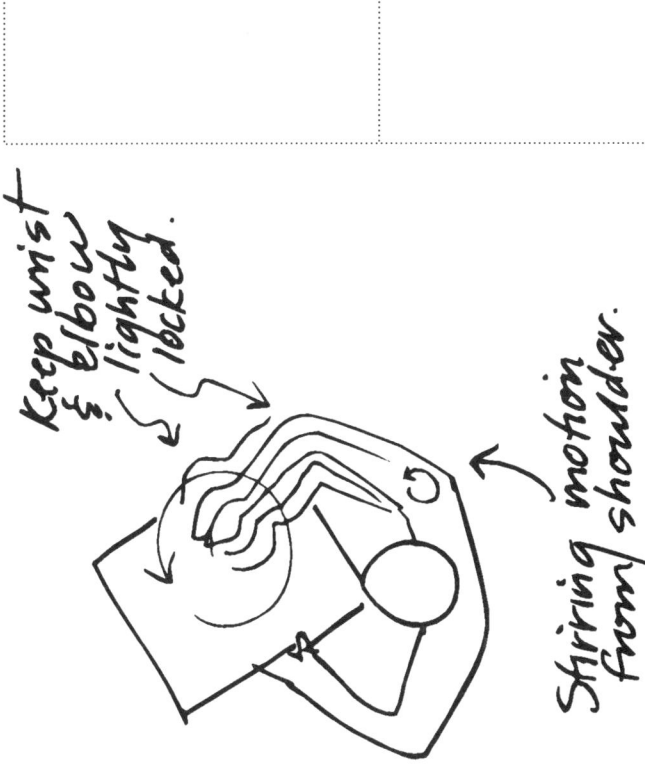

TIP *Circle around a few times before touching down to the paper.*

27 *Your Body Knows!*

Expanding Circles

Repeat the circle exercise. Make each one bigger and bigger.

CENTER

- Continue perching over the table, with arm hanging and circling from the shoulder.
- Keep wrist and elbow lightly locked.

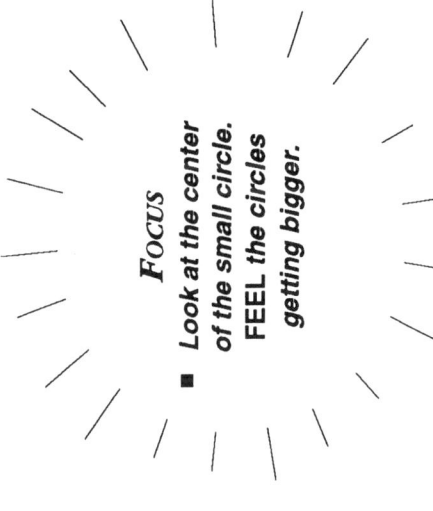

FOCUS

- **Look at the center of the small circle. FEEL the circles getting bigger.**

DRAW

- Draw without moving your focus.

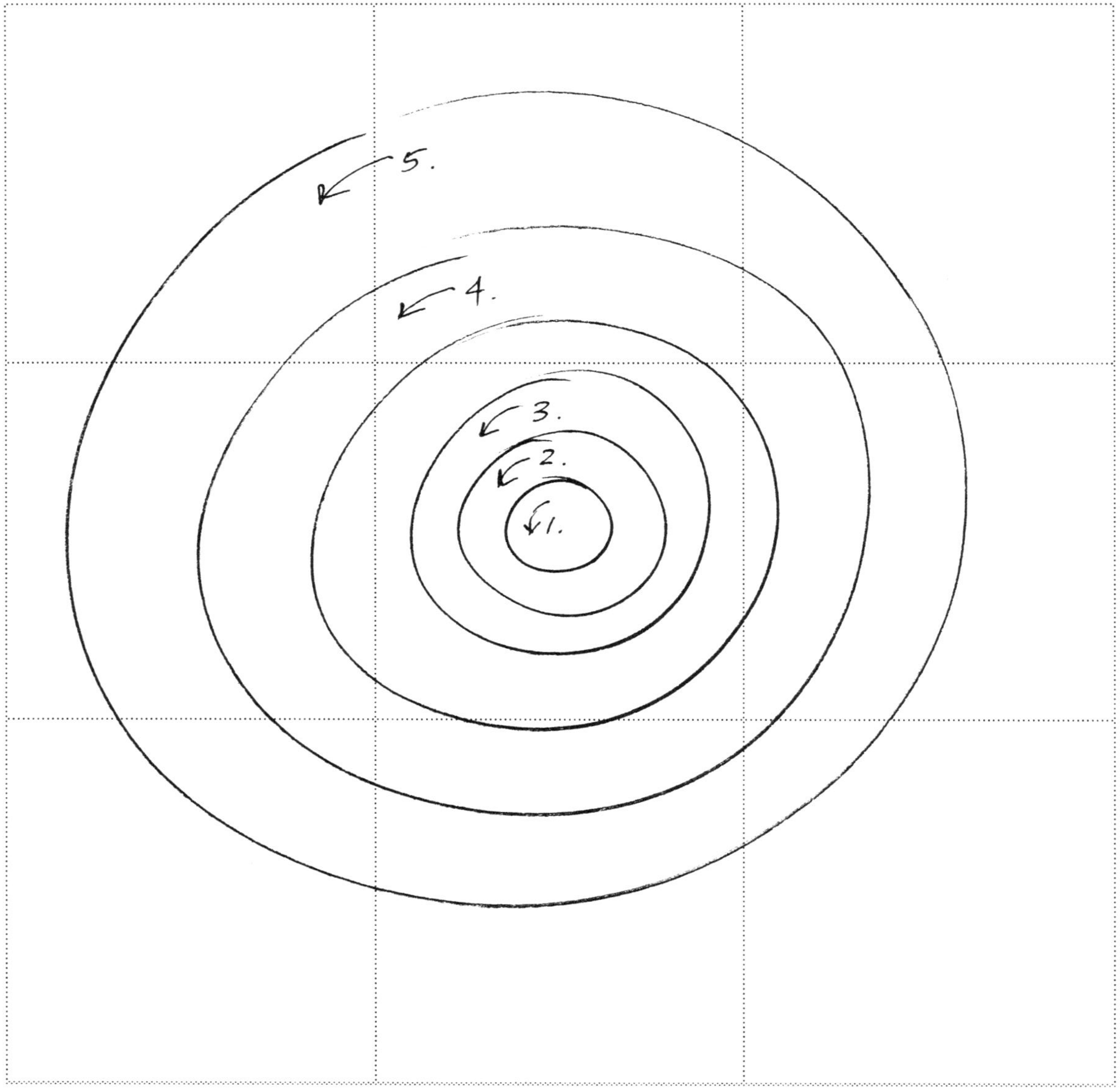

Who's the ace?

Oh, the town fool. He shoots up the wall & paints targets on the holes.

TIP You can start big and give yourself the instruction to get small.

Spirals

Center
- Balance.
- Lock your wrist and elbow, and let your arm hang loosely from your shoulder.

Focus
- Feel your arm stirring in a small circle then tell yourself "BIGGER."

Draw
- Touch down and let your circling expand.

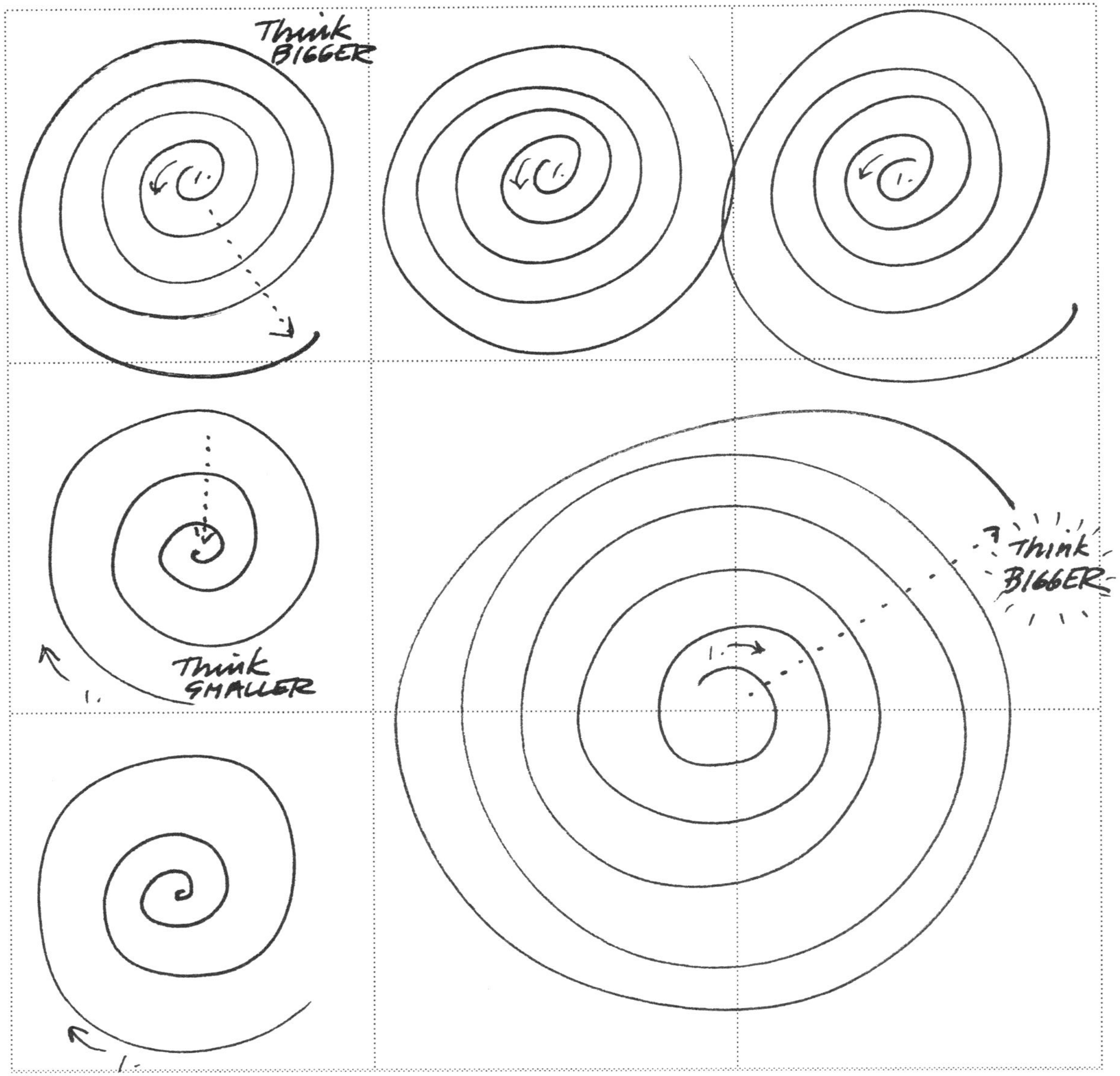

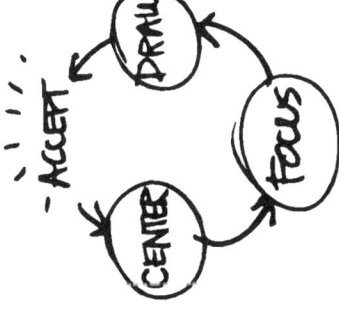

TIP *The simple line curled on itself suggests a dynamic relationship of unity. Through the ages the spiral has symbolized evolution and transformation.*

Your Body Knows!

Curves

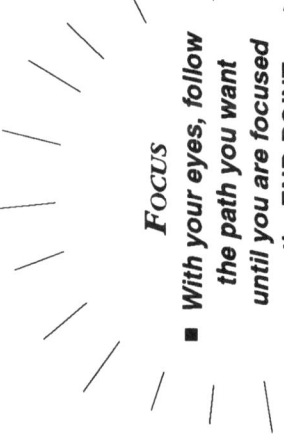

Center
- Balance.
- Loosen your body.
- Set pen at the start of the line.

Focus
- With your eyes, follow the path you want until you are focused on the END POINT.

Draw
- Throw the line, letting your felt image of the visual journey guide your line.
- Repeat, staying focused on the end point and the feeling.
- Repeat with closed eyes.

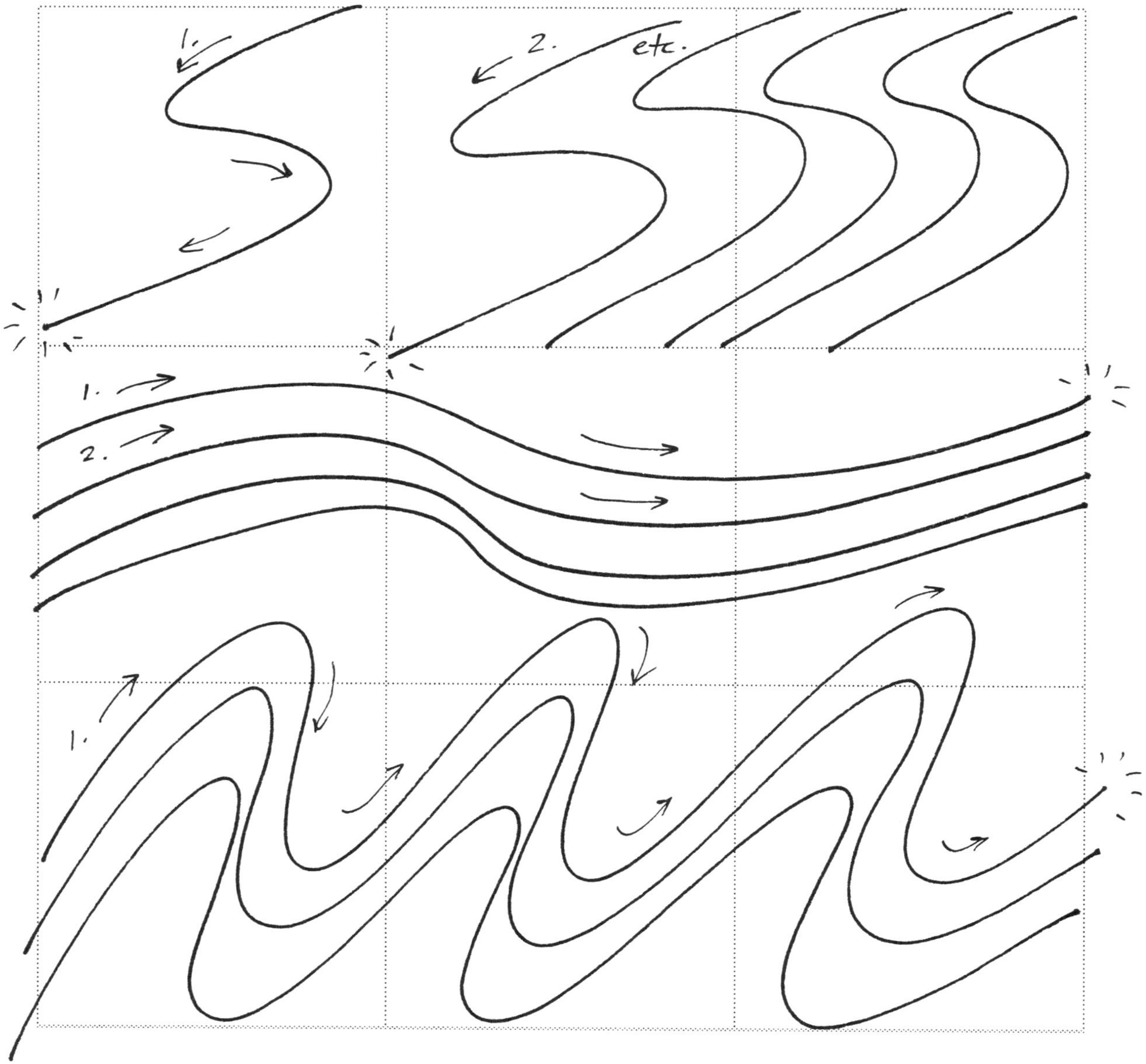

TIP *You will experience your body "remembering" the throw lines as you repeat them.*

An amazing fact is that we remember the movement in both directions. So you can both throw a curve and retrace it by simply instructing yourself to "go back to the beginning."

33 *Your Body Knows!*

©1993 Graphic Guides Inc.

Combinations

- This swooping arrow is a combination of curves and throw lines.
- Follow the steps shown in each box.

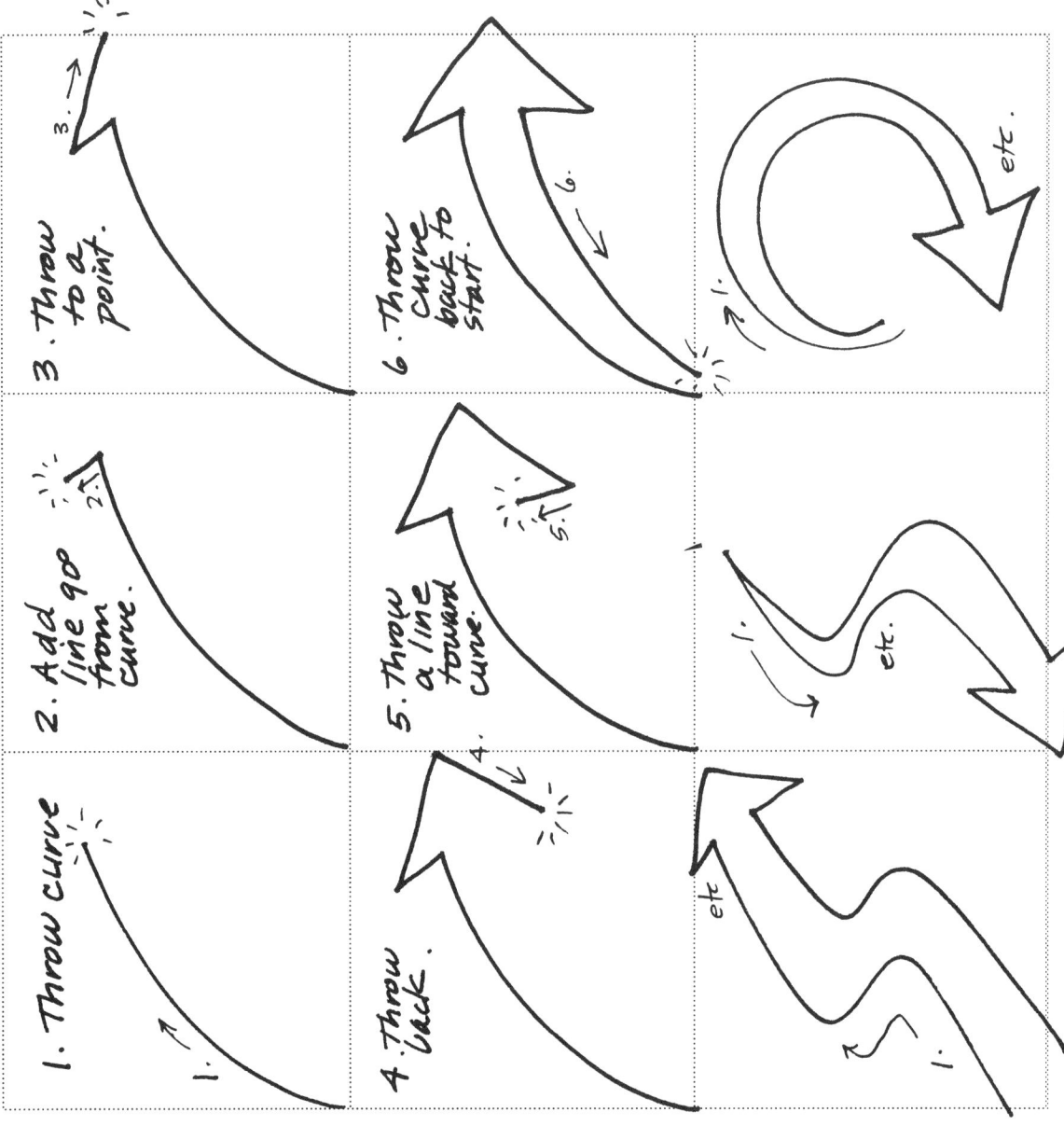

TIP *Call upon your entire mind/body/spirit for drawing and leave behind analytical thought.*

34 *Your Body Knows!*

So that's how it's done!

TIP *Your body can easily draw mirror images if you hold a pen in each hand and draw at the same time.*

Your Body Knows!

CHAPTER 4

Lettering

BASIC STROKES

L ETTERS ARE ALL COMPOSED OF THE BASIC STROKES YOU'VE JUST LEARNED. There are only *five* strokes in all.

Practicing Letters

Basic letter strokes

All these letters use *drop* lines and *horizon* lines.

These use *diagonal* lines, *horizon* lines, and *drop* lines.

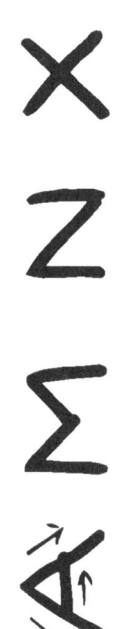

And all these letters use *circles* as a base.

Consistency of lettering comes from:

1. **CENTERING** in a balanced way as you write, holding your wrist lightly locked.

2. **FOCUSING** on *each* stroke as a separate throw line or circle.

3. **DRAWING** using "muscle memory" so you literally draw all similar strokes on the same angle or curve.

©1993 Graphic Guides Inc.

Block letters

Each row of the practice grids in this chapter has a letter with stroke order indicated. Remember to:

- Repeat the letter in each box.
- Work for consistency.
- Go slowly until the stroke order is second nature.
- Make sure horizon lines are parallel to the top edge and at 90 degrees to your forearm.

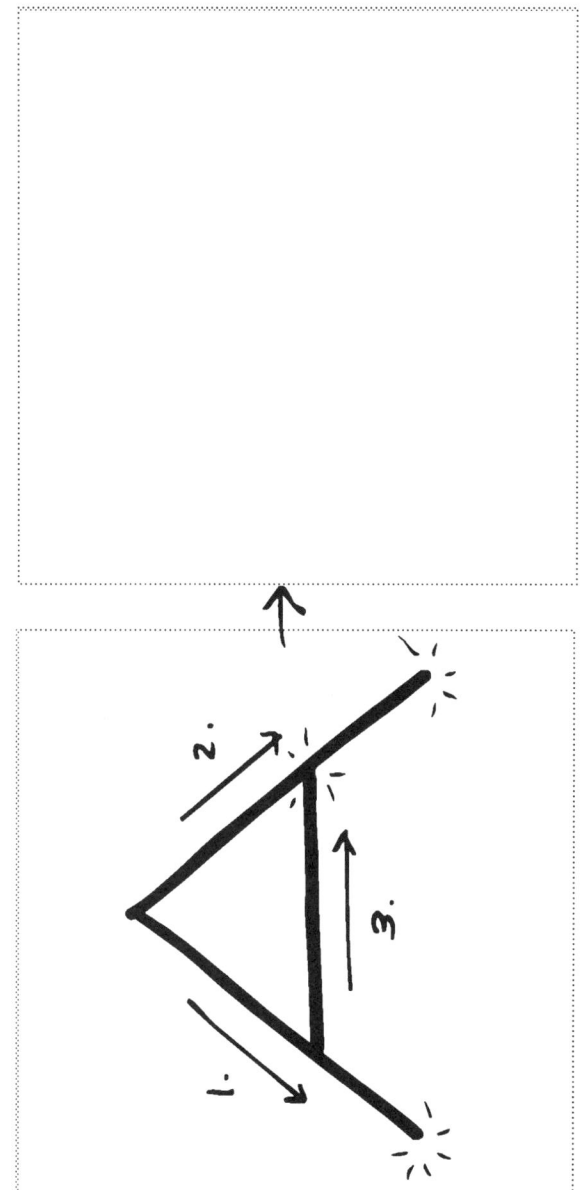

and Practice! Practice! Practice!

Alphabet Grouped by Stroke

- **Use droplines and horizon lines.**

TIP *Keep your wrist lightly locked. Draw with your whole arm.*

40 *Lettering*

© 1993 Graphic Guides Inc.

■ **Add diagonal lines.**

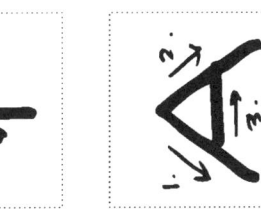   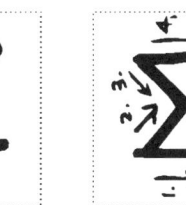  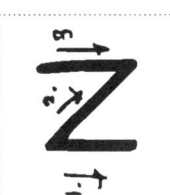 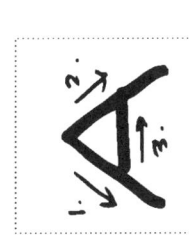    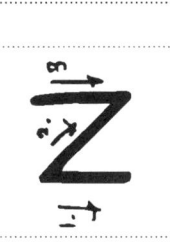

Throw

Pull

Alphabet Grouped by Stroke

Are you sitting centered?

TIP *Accept your own style and body architecture, and sit there firmly. Infinite possibilities extend from that center.*

■ **Feel the circles.**

 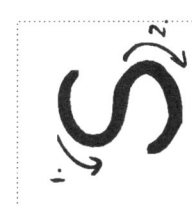 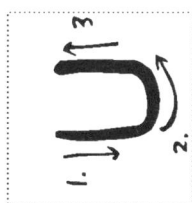 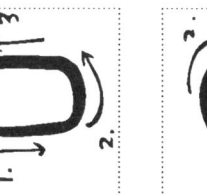 

Alphabet Grouped by Stroke

- **Combine straight and curved.**

TIP *Think of letters as small buildings constructed of these basic lines. Be thoughtful as you draw them on your landscape.*

Lower Case Alphabet

- Keep the "circle" focus strong with small letters.

Center Focus Draw!

46   Lettering

©1993 Graphic Guides Inc.

TIP Use a neutral, darker color for regular lettering and other colors for titling and emphasis.

Lower Case Alphabet

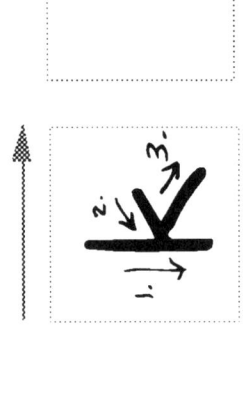

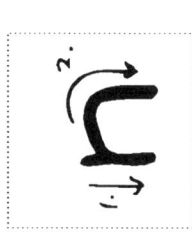
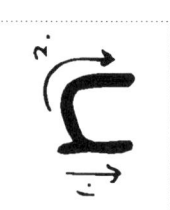
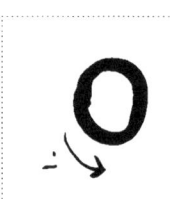

TIP *The secret to clear lower case letters is a consistent dropline.*

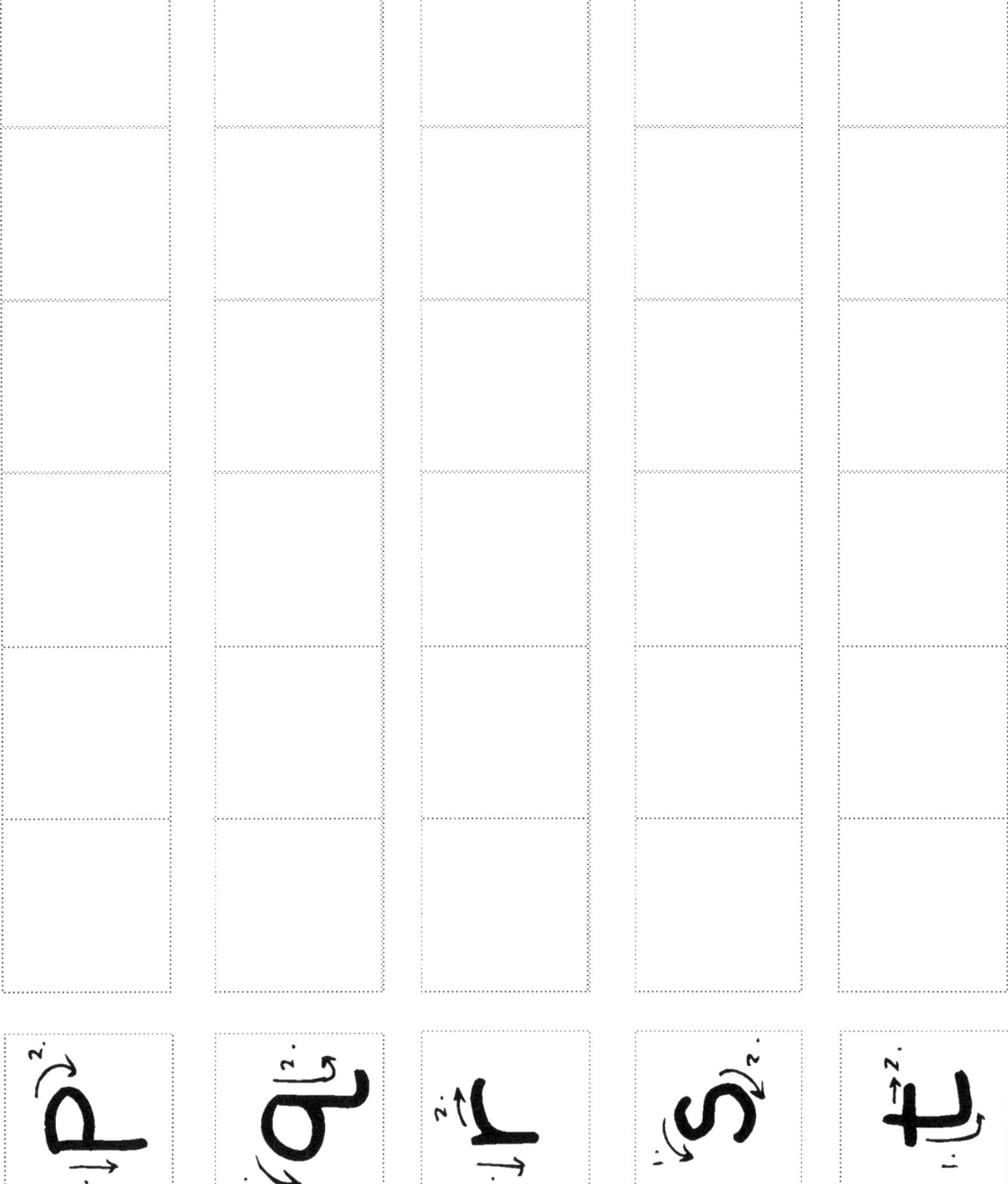

Lower Case Alphabet

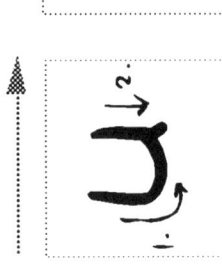   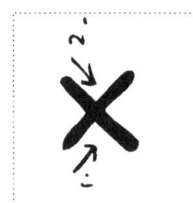 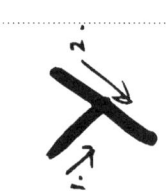

TIP *Acceptance is just that—complete trust that what your body draws is honest and truthful.*

↑

| 1.↑ N ↓2. ↑3. | write your name → | write other words → | | |

TIP Use upper case for chart titles, lower case for other words.

Lettering

Numbers

- Numbers use the same basic strokes.

    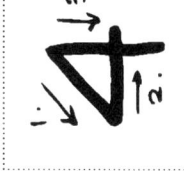

TIP *Draw with your heart open.*

CHAPTER 5

Seed Shapes

EED SHAPES ARE SIMPLE GRAPHIC IMAGES. They are called "seed shapes" because they have the ability to grow and elaborate without changing the original drawing. Each seed shape reflects the essence of a pattern found in the visual world. The seed shapes shown here form a basic vocabulary for graphic language.

As language is organized with nouns and verbs to create increasingly complex levels of expression—sentences, paragraphs, stories, and novels—the seven basic seed shapes can be organized to represent an increasingly complex level of expression.

Pictographs are little pictures of physical things

PICTOGRAPHS ARE SMALL PICTURES OF REAL THINGS—REAL PHYSICAL THINGS, THAT IS. They are the little pictures of birds and trees, flip charts and people—the adjectives and objects of graphic language.

Stroke order is an important part of a seed shape used as language. One does not want to have spend any more time on basic shapes than one spends on basic words. The creativity is in the elaboration and combination. Learning basic stroke orders lets your body do the work where your mind is making meaning.

Ideographs are symbolic pictures of non-physical things

IDEOGRAPHS ARE SMALL SYMBOLIC DRAWINGS THAT MAY NOT NECESSARILY RESEMBLE WHAT THEY REPRESENT. A heart for instance doesn't look like "love" but is a common symbol for it. The first seven shapes are the simplest patterns one can draw, organized into an easy-to-remember sequence. At an archetypal level they have a common meaning drawn from the way it feels to create them. At a symbolic level, they can represent many different things, depending on what words are attached to them. These seven little "seed shapes" form a simple keyboard for graphic language. They function a little like verbs in graphic language used for group communication. One set of meanings is suggested here. Many others are layered on top through different usage.

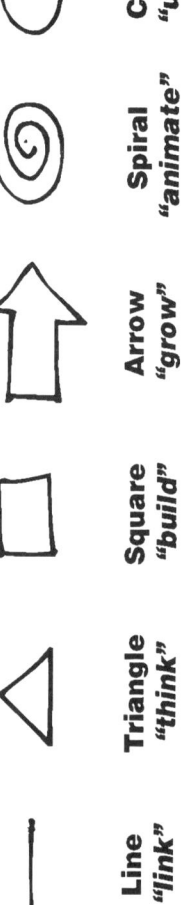

©1993 Graphic Guides Inc.

56   Seed Shapes

Follow the stroke order

Each seed shape is illustrated in the manner shown below. Practice involves repeating the shape slowly until you know the stroke order and can execute each stroke as a separate little line that is "thrown" or "felt" into being. Additional repetitions then build the basic shape into "muscle memory." Once memorized, elaborations can be added easily.

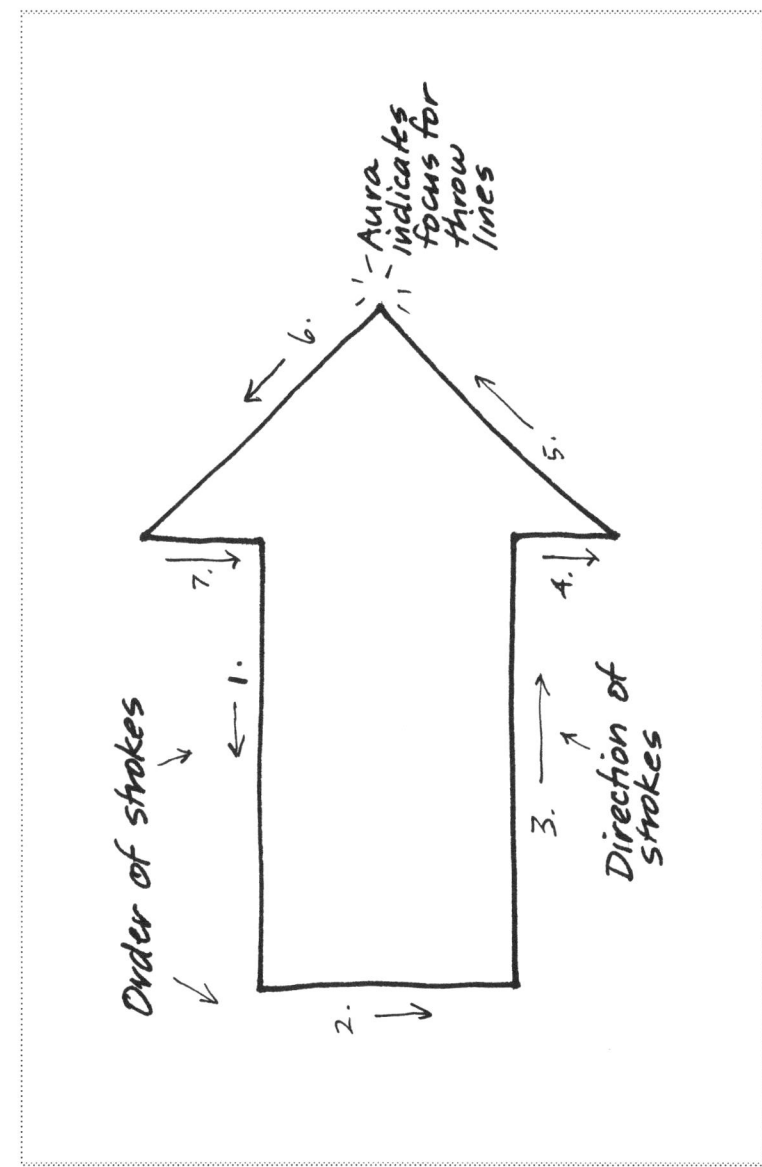

Seed Shapes/Point

■ Review the stroke order of the seed points illustrated below. Points focus attention. They mean "look here."

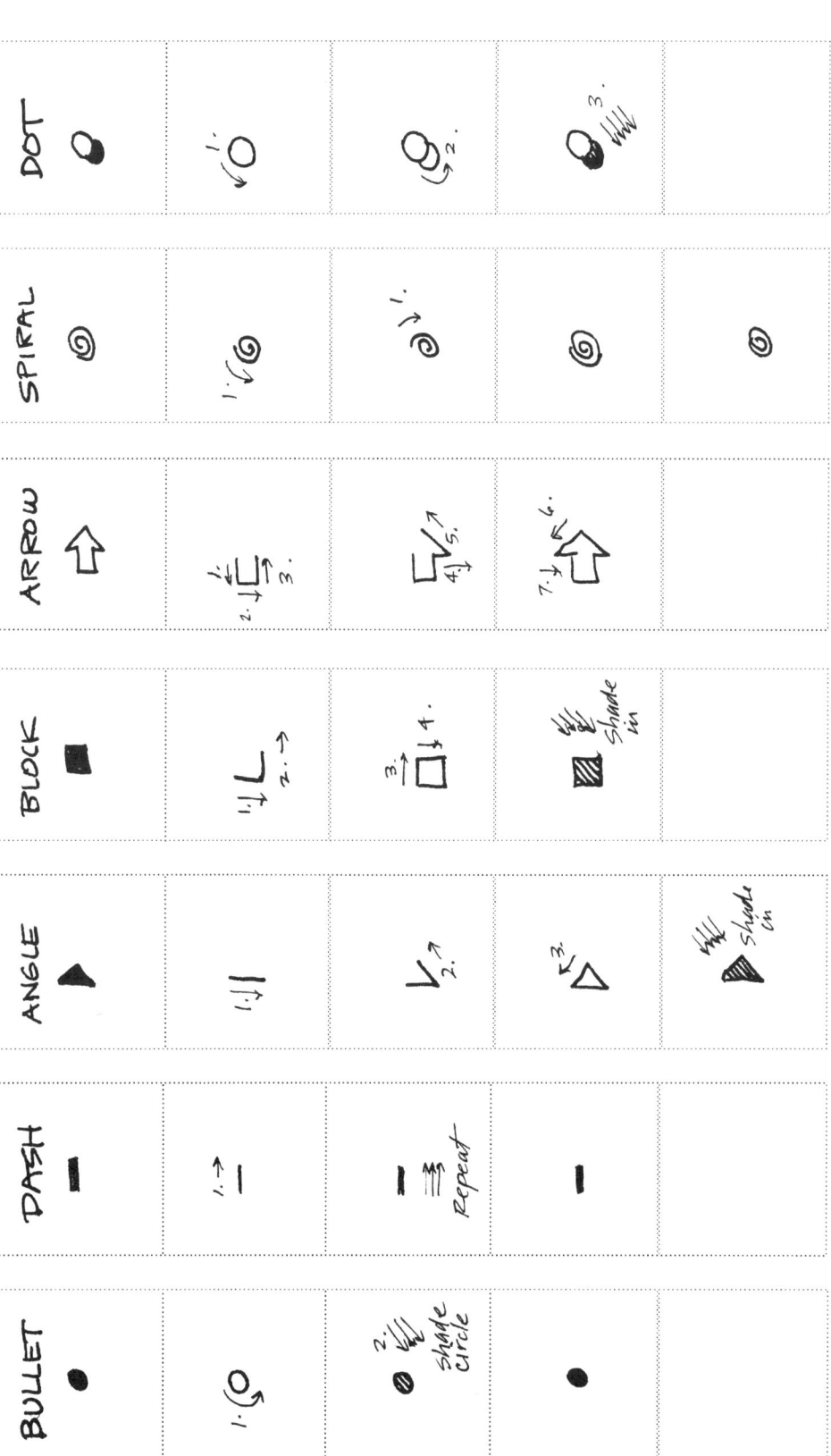

58 Seed Shapes

- **Now draw each shape five times (or more if you like) until the stroke order is automatic.**

Seed Shapes/Line

- **Note the stroke order of the seed lines below. Lines indicate relationship between points, either connecting or separating. The pattern and thickness of the line can suggest types of relationships.**

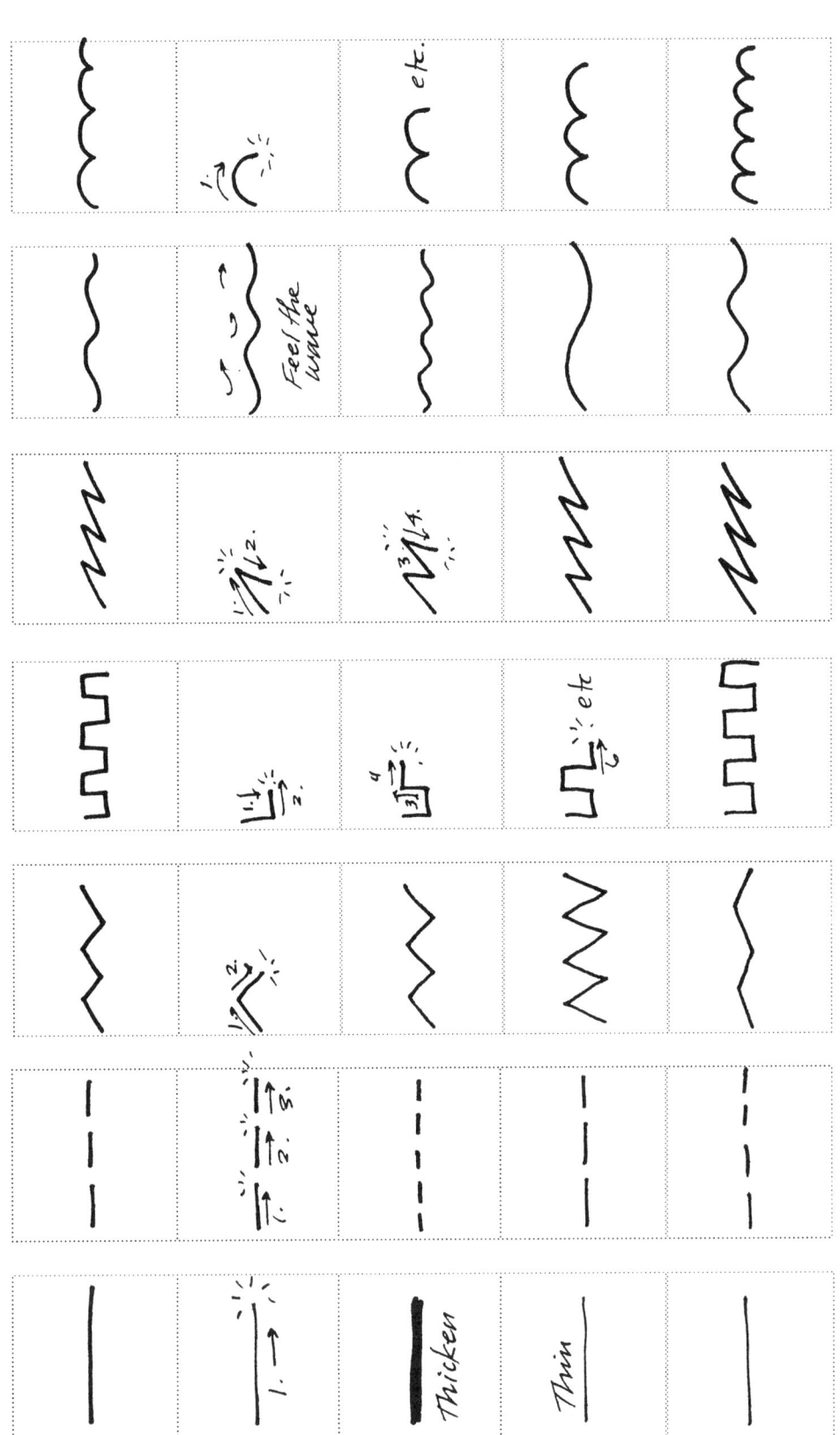

TIP *Getting off the line and looking at it is the first act of consciousness.*

60 Seed Shapes

■ **Now draw each type of line, picking up speed as you repeat it.**

Seed Shapes/Triangle

- Triangles begin with the base. Then lines are "thrown" to the point and back to the base. Angles define space, create the first simple shapes, and are very active visually.

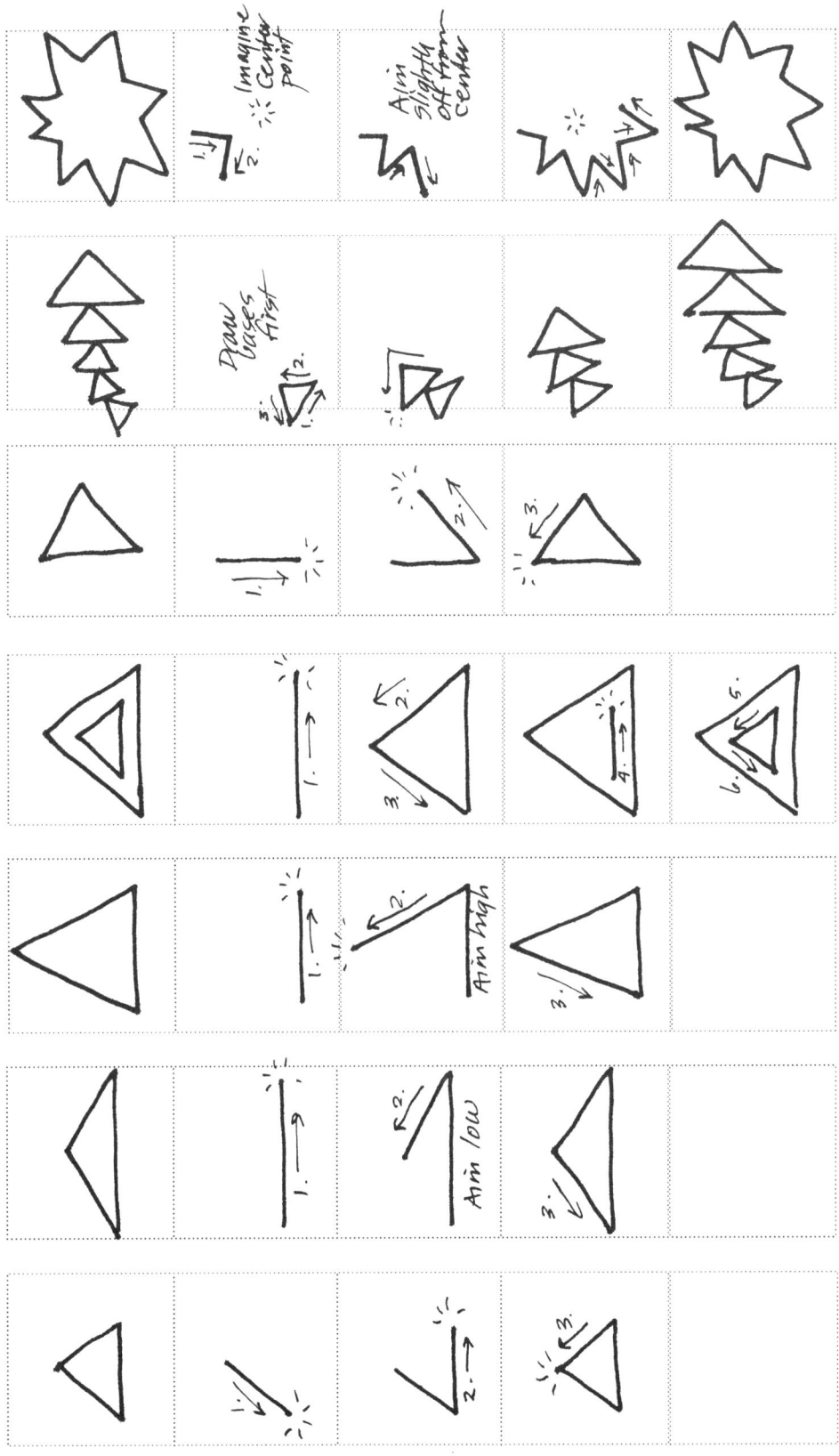

Seed Shapes

■ **Draw each shape as quickly as you can!**

TIP *In navigation, triangulation is the key to location. To pin something down—to know where you are—you need to get an angle on it.*

63 *Seed Shapes*

©1993 Graphic Guides Inc.

Seed Shapes/Square

- Neat squares are drawn using "muscle memory" from the first two strokes (i.e. drop line, horizon line—horizon line, drop line). They can also be drawn going around one stroke at a time. Their formal organization is great for representing anything that's highly structured.

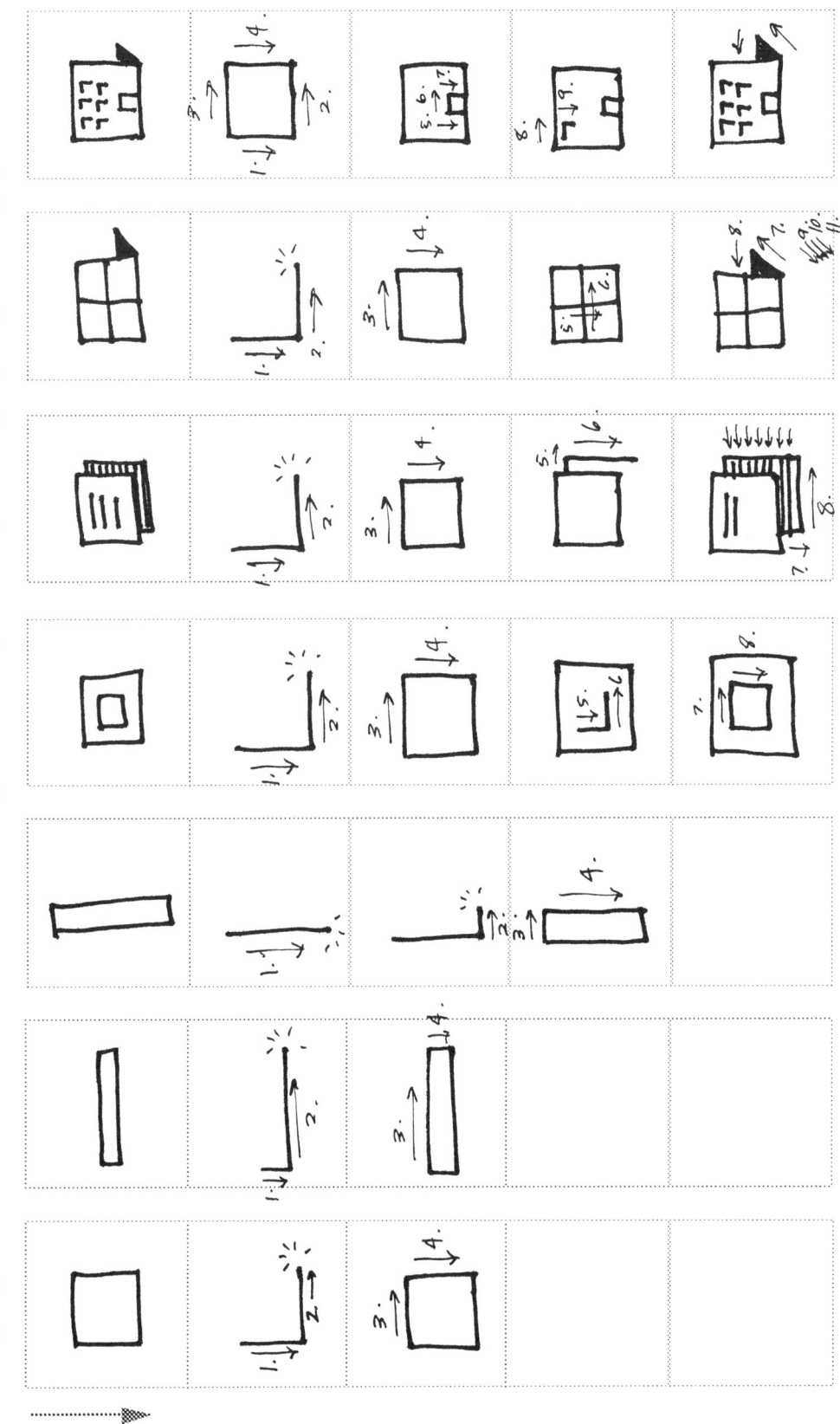

■ **Draw little squares first, then get bigger.**

TIP *Squares suggest solid organization, and anything with clearly connected parts—formal organizations, buildings, documents.*

Seed Shapes

©1993 Graphic Guides Inc.

Seed Shapes/Hollow Arrow

- Arrows begin as squares and break into triangles at the end of stroke #3. These shapes are great for indicating projects that "fly," "drive," "stretch" etc. Write the name of the project on the arrow.

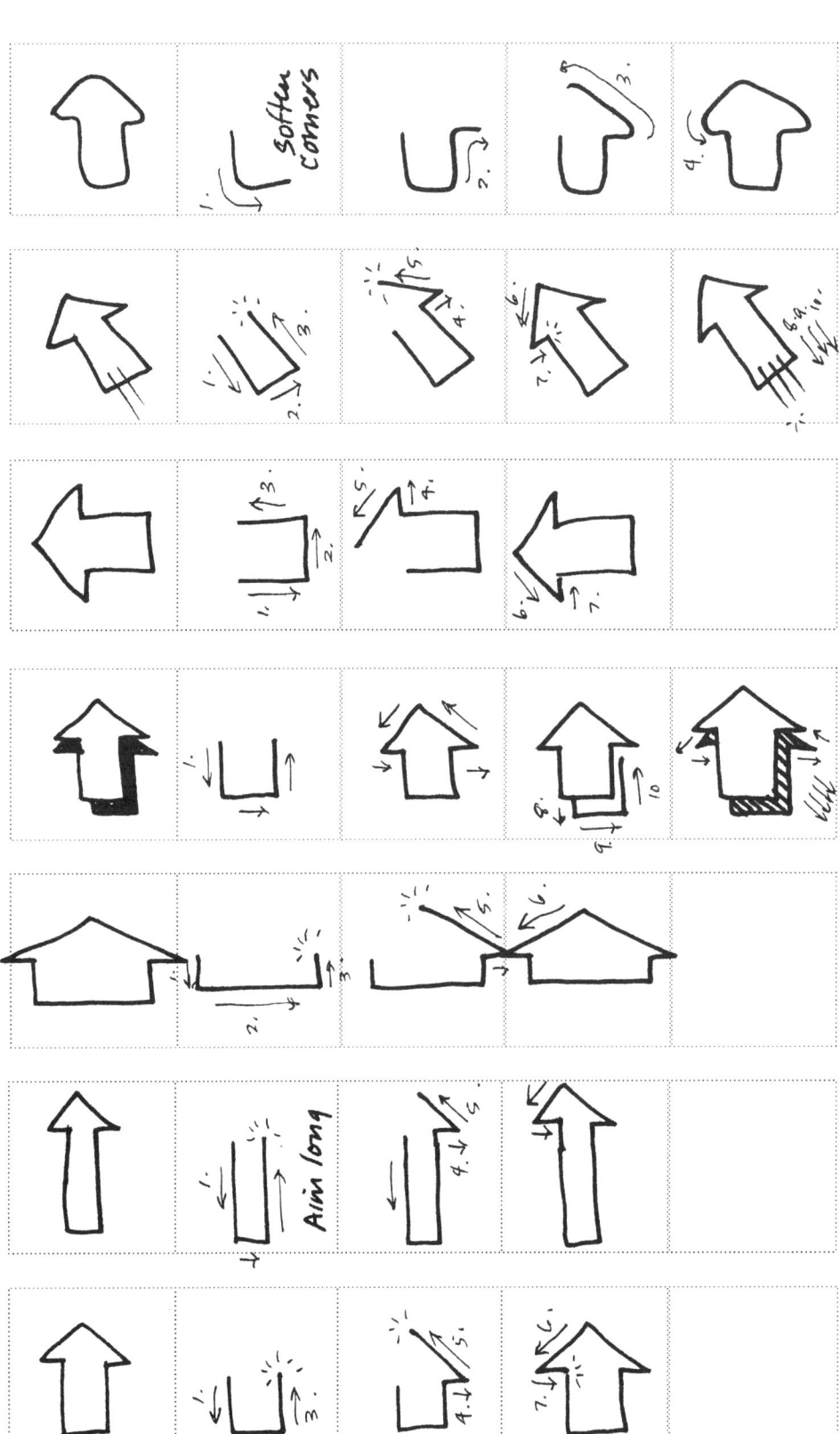

■ **Fill these squares with arrows aiming in different directions.**

TIP *The arrow unfailingly points to activity in one direction and depicts an organized action or project—projects, progress, task forces, political forces.*

Seed Shapes/Spiral

- Spirals are *very* flexible. When you focus mostly on the circular feeling, the snailing shapes indicate dynamic unity. When you focus on curves, the more snaky lines represent dynamic forces like wind, public opinion, and change.

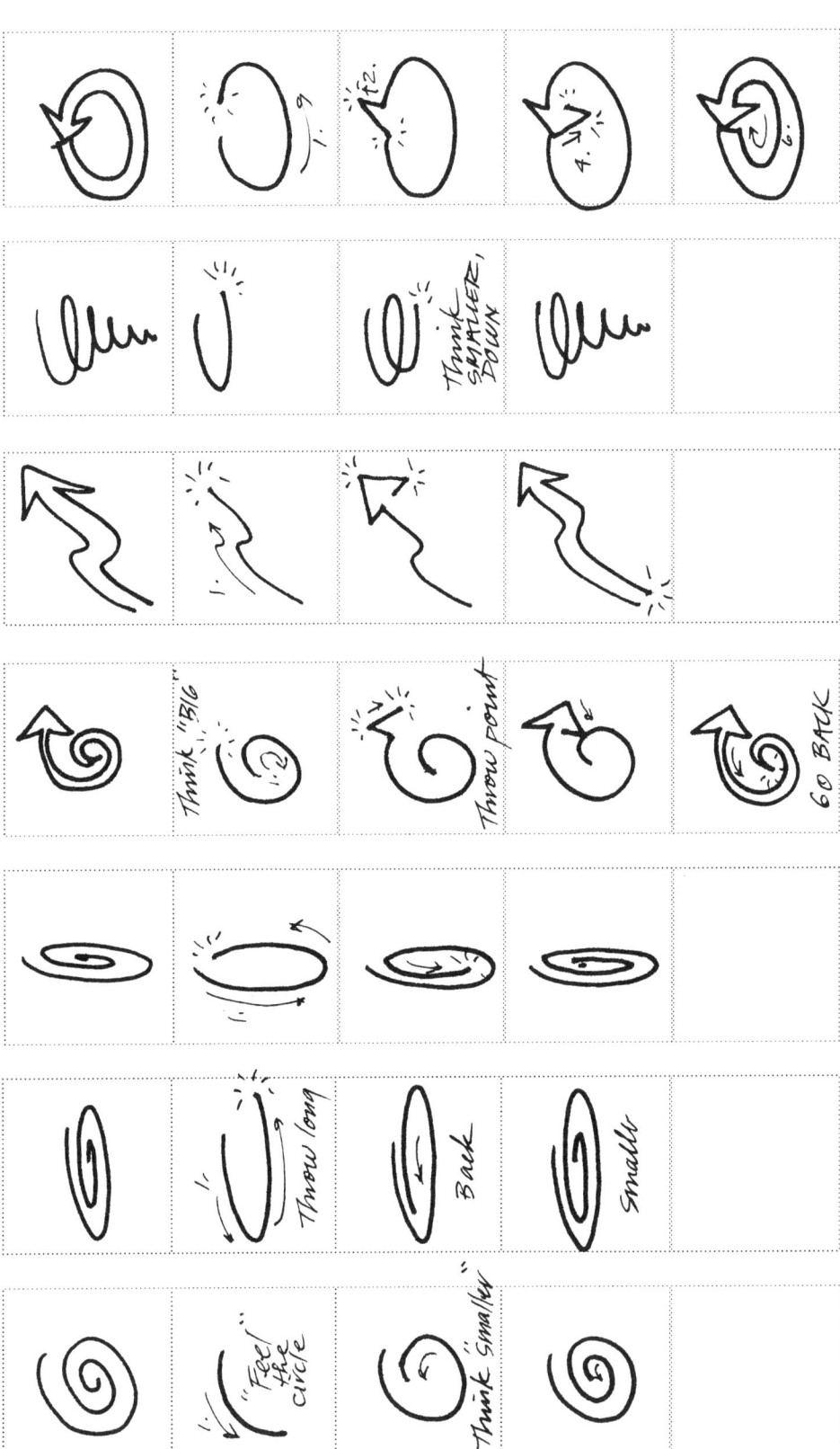

■ **Repeat the shapes illustrated above.**

TIP *When you focus, you are letting one image or phenomenon fill you completely until it overflows as a drawing.*

Seed Shapes

Seed Shapes/Circle

■ The circle indicates unity as an ideograph and is useful for all kinds of pictographs.

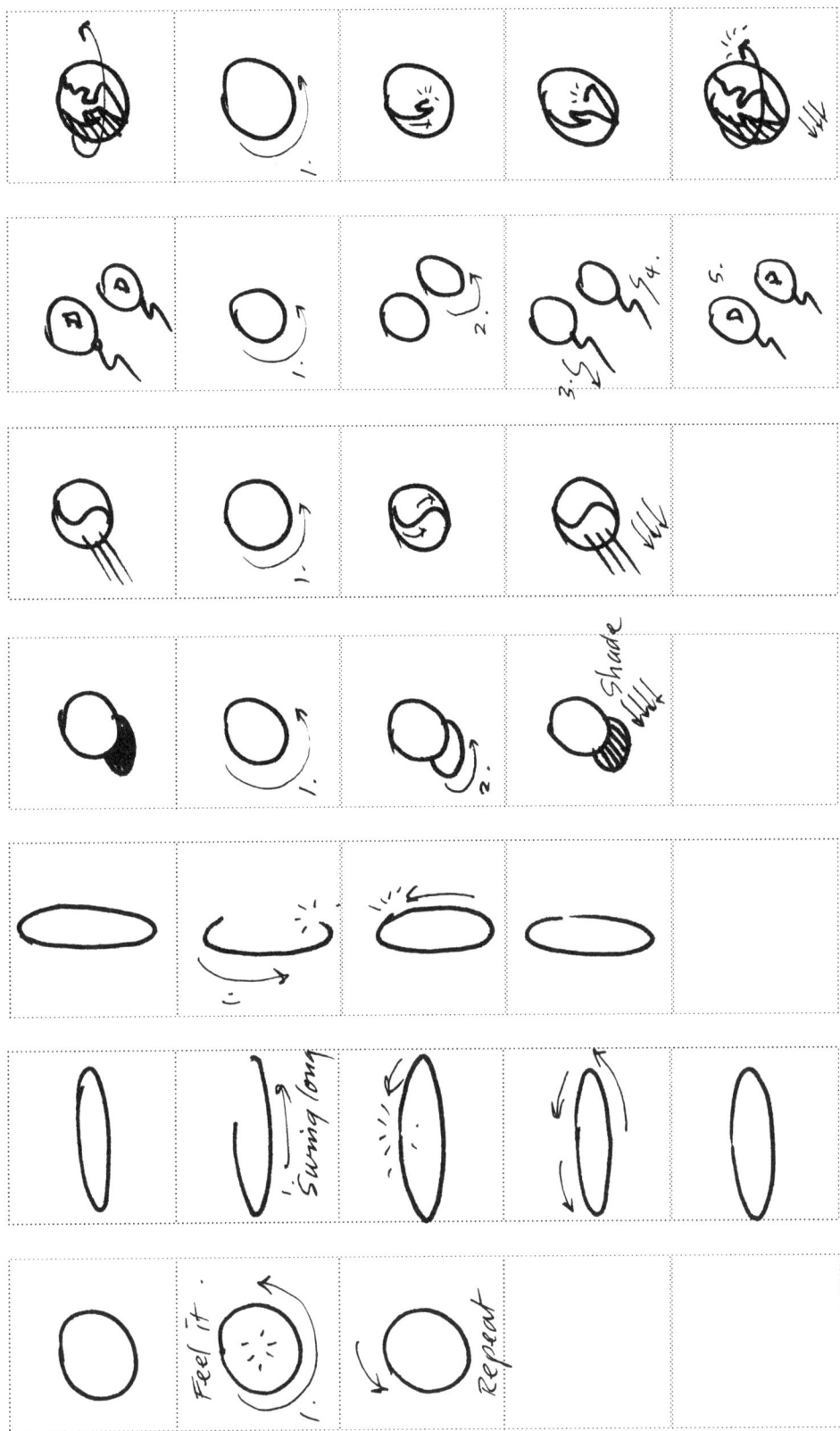

Seed Shapes

- **Reproduce the drawings above.**

TIP *The circle is unity the world over—an inclusive symbol—wholes, committees, teams, meetings, individuals, mom, earth, head, eyes.*

Line Improvisations

- Repeat the drawings shown below.
  Each builds on seed shapes.

Ocean

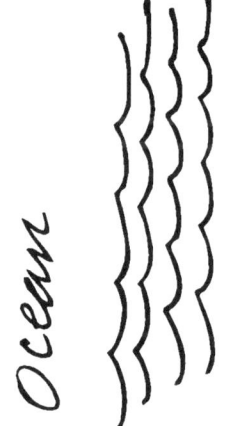

stream

star

72 Seed Shapes

Making a Point with Auras

Starburst

- **Throw from center out.**

aura

- **Throw from outside in.**

NAME

- **Throw top ones in, bottom ones out.**

Seed Shapes

Line Objects

Pencil
1. →
2. →
3. →

Marker
- Draw barrel rectangle first.

Paper
1. →
2. →
3. →

74 Seed Shapes

©1993 Graphic Guides Inc.

Birds

- Use muscle memory to repeat wings. Focus on "smaller."

Book

- Start with three birds.

Road

- Draw away from the "vanishing point."

Seed Shapes

Angles

Mountains

- Throw the top of a triangle.

Plus road

- Add curves from vanishing point.

- Add aura.

76 Seed Shapes

©1993 Graphic Guides Inc.

■ **Improvise.**

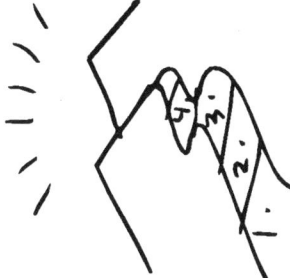

Seed Shapes

Triangles

- **Build from triangle.**

house

trees

Hourglass

Time Cones

BANG

79 Seed Shapes

Rectangles

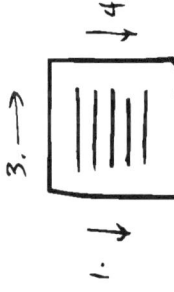

Memo

- Use muscle memory to repeat stroke 2 on stroke 3. This increases the chance they'll be parallel.

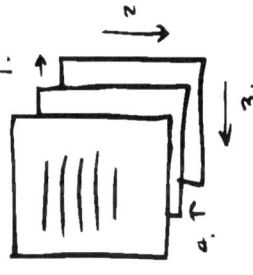

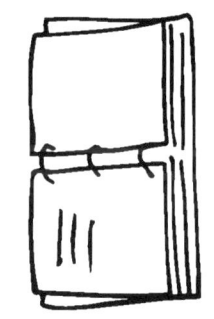

Ring binder

Video

Computer

Radio

- **Do keys as little "L's."**

81 Seed Shapes

The Diamond

- **Use muscle memory to get parallel lines.**

- **Draw bottom lines toward the center.**

- **Draw curved droplines after diamond.**

Leaves

Box

- Use drop lines. Make the middle stroke (6) longer.

File

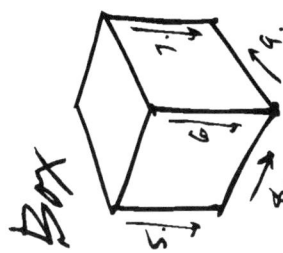

Seed Shapes

Boxes From Diamonds

- Draw the diamond first.

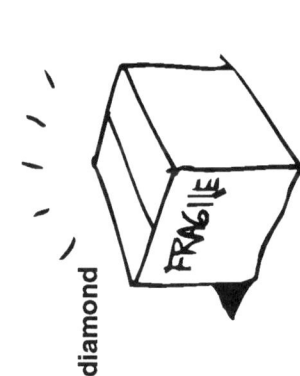

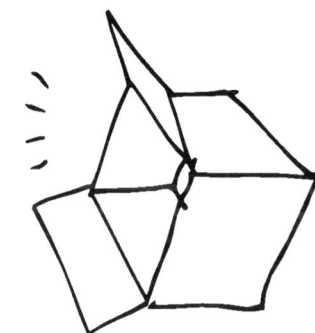
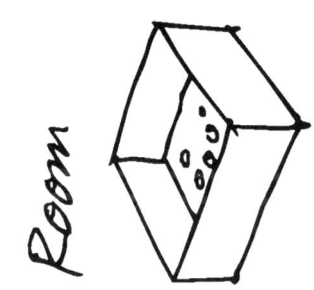

- **Draw the diamond first.**

Table

Grid

Concrete

©1993 Graphic Guides Inc.

Buildings (More Rectangles Plus Angles)

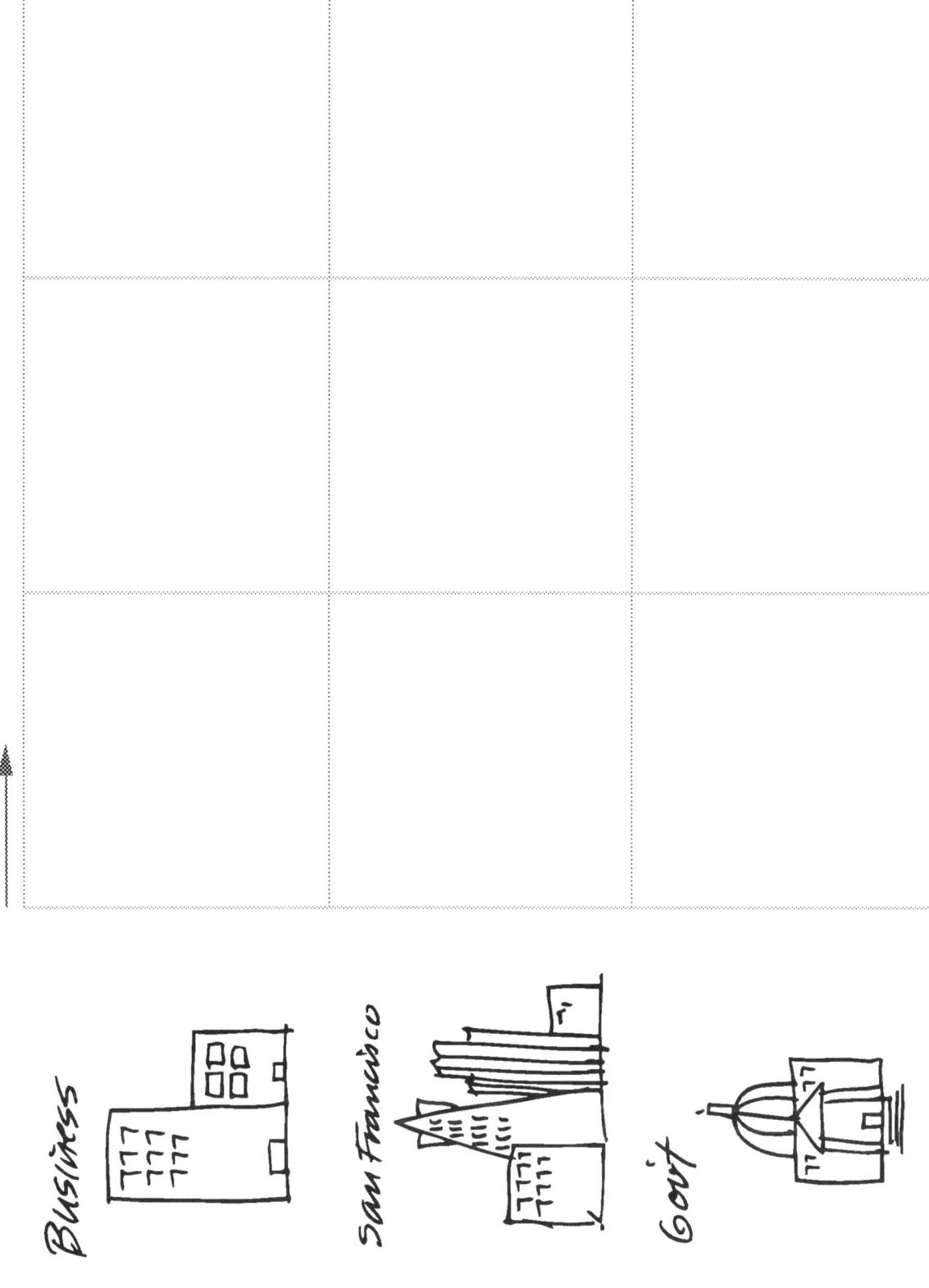

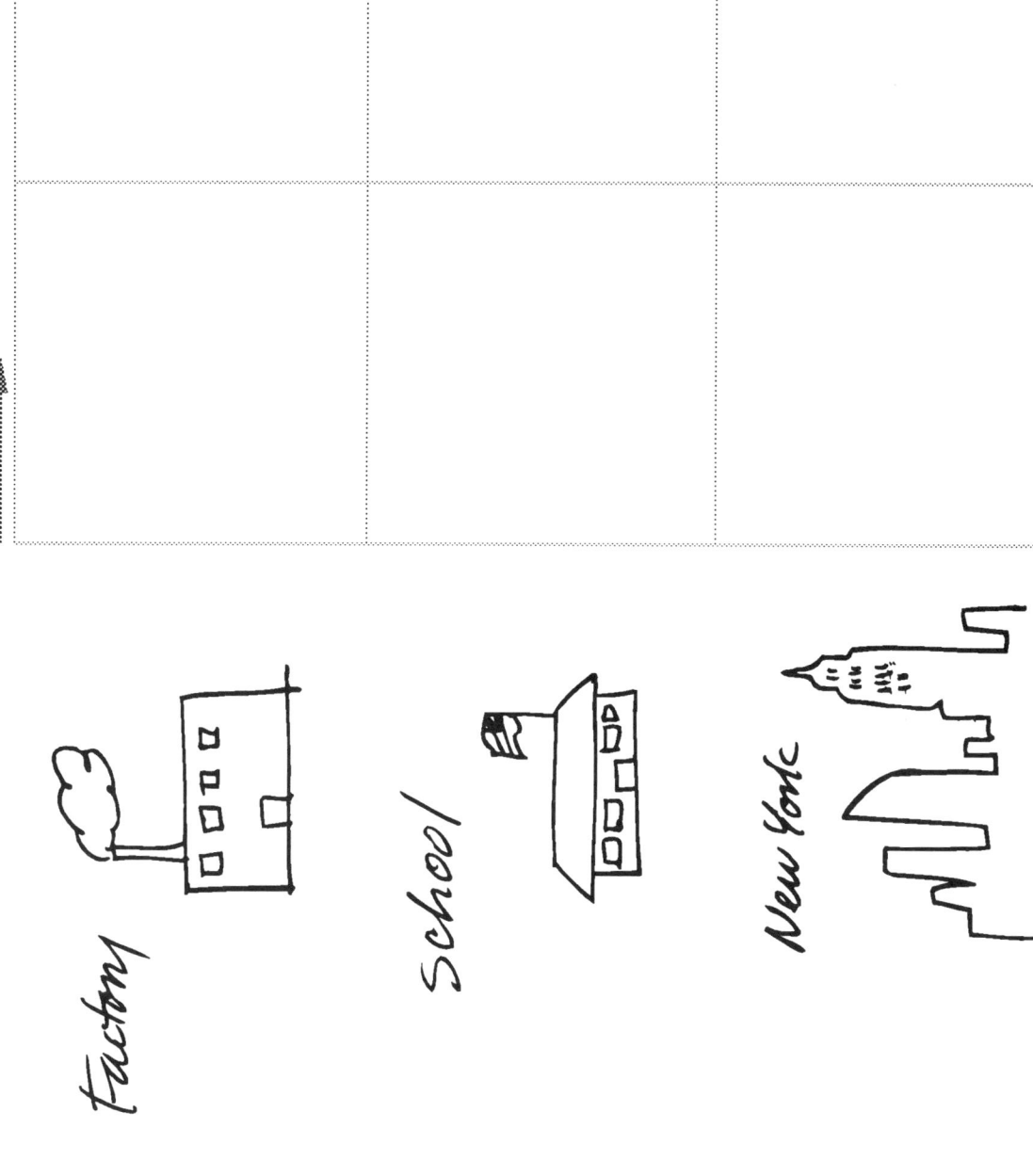

Media (Rectangles, Parallelograms)

- **Use a lazy "H" as the seed shape.**

  Flip Chart

- **Start with a square.**

  Screen
  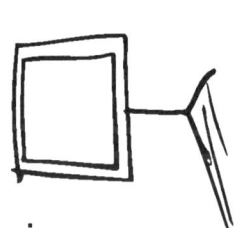

  Over head
  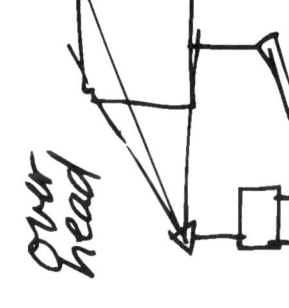

copy board

video

Telephone

Shapes in Perspective

- **Start from long diamond.**

wall

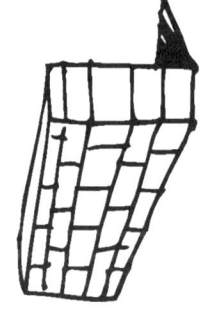

Industrial Park

- **Draw houses first.**

Arrows

- Begin with the hollow arrow.

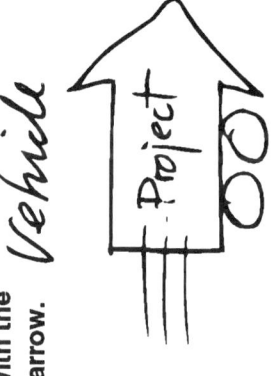
Vehicle / Project

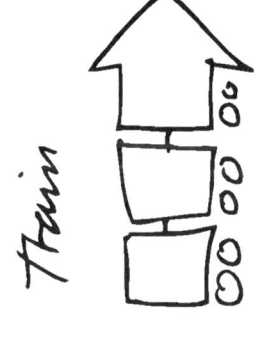
Train

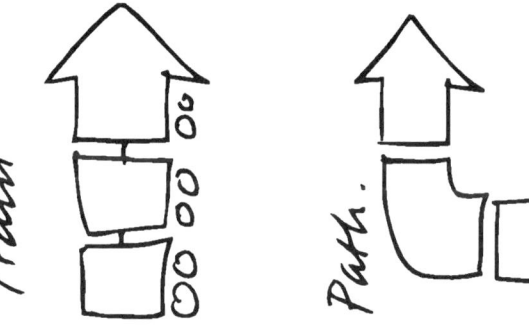
Path

Seed Shapes

More Arrows

- Throw long lines toward and away from a vanishing point.

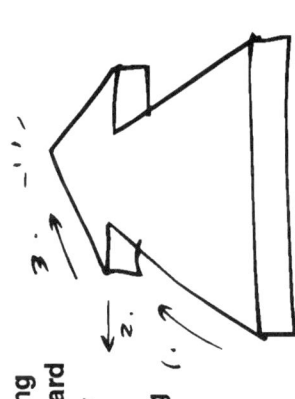 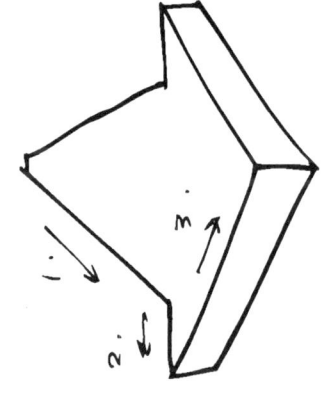 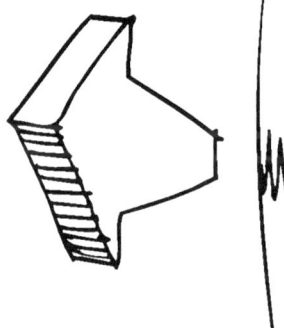

Flight of projects

Project
777
project

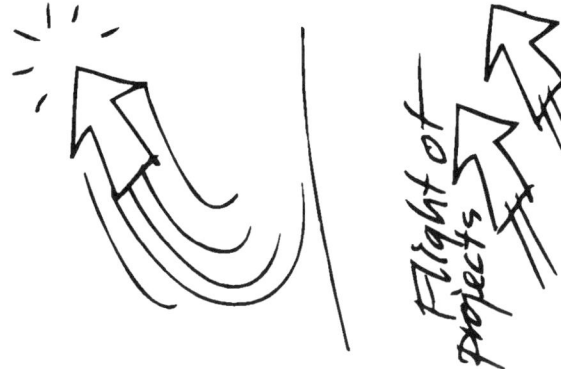

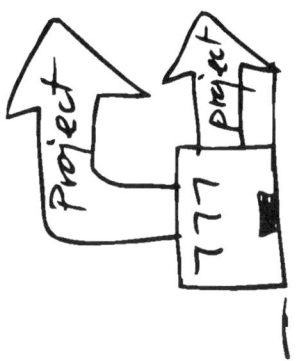

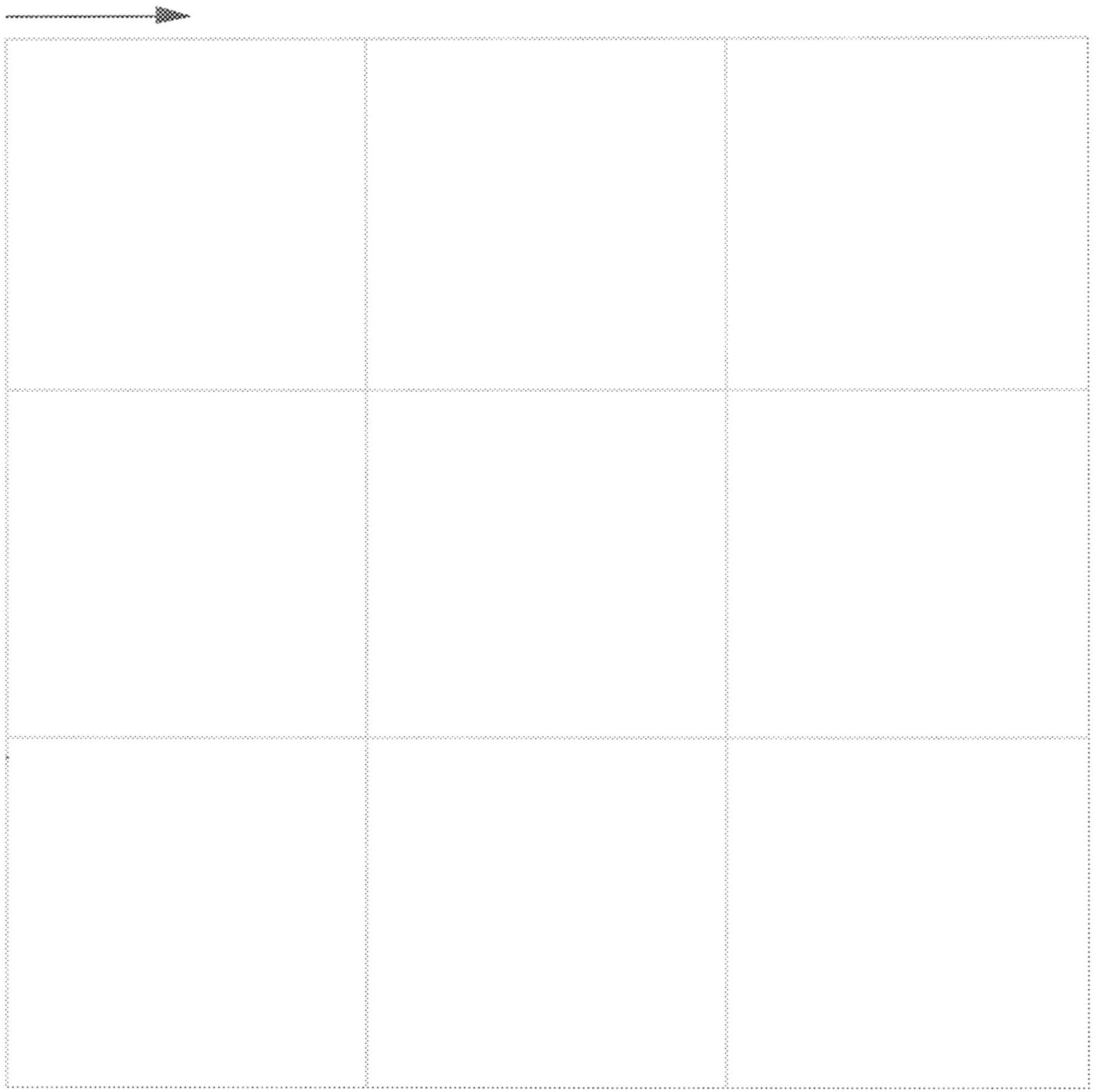

Dynamic Shapes

- Draw a spiral and hop over the space where the second spiral line goes.

Spiral

- **Draw parallelograms first.**

- **Lift off by phase.**

Seed Shapes

More Spirals and Curves

rope

maypole

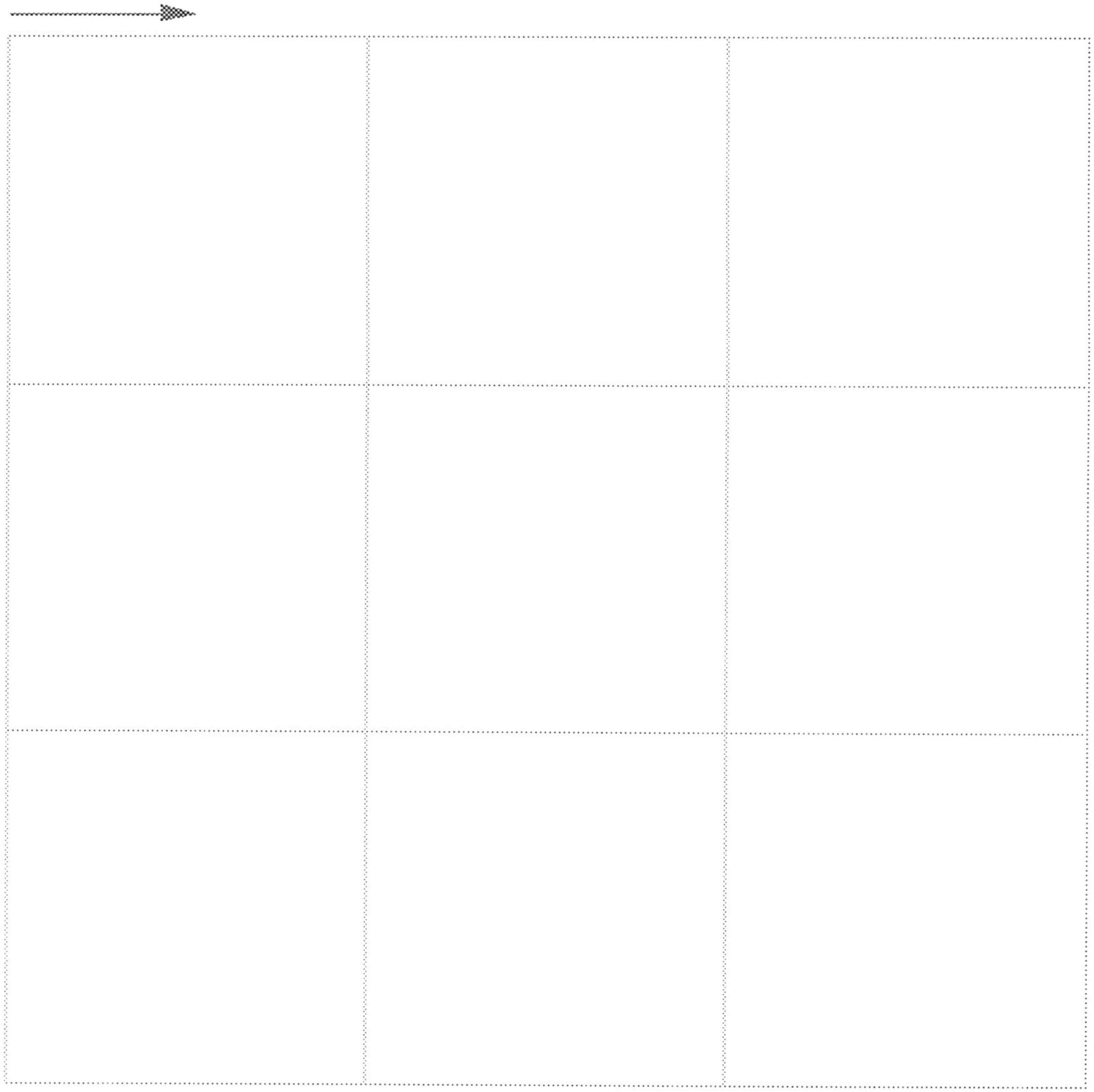

Seed Shapes

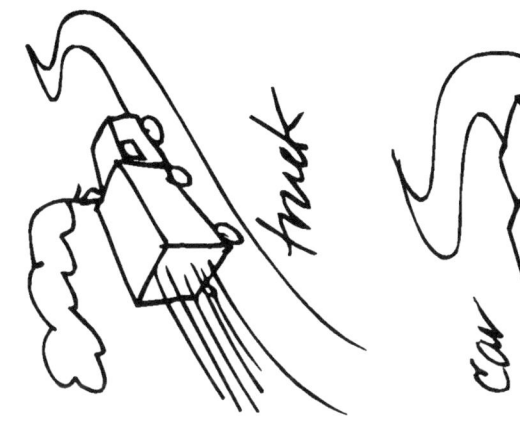

Full Circle

- **Curve wrap-around lines downward to make viewer feel "above" the ball.**

- **Curve lines up to make viewer feel beneath the balloon.**

Ball

Balloon

Parachute

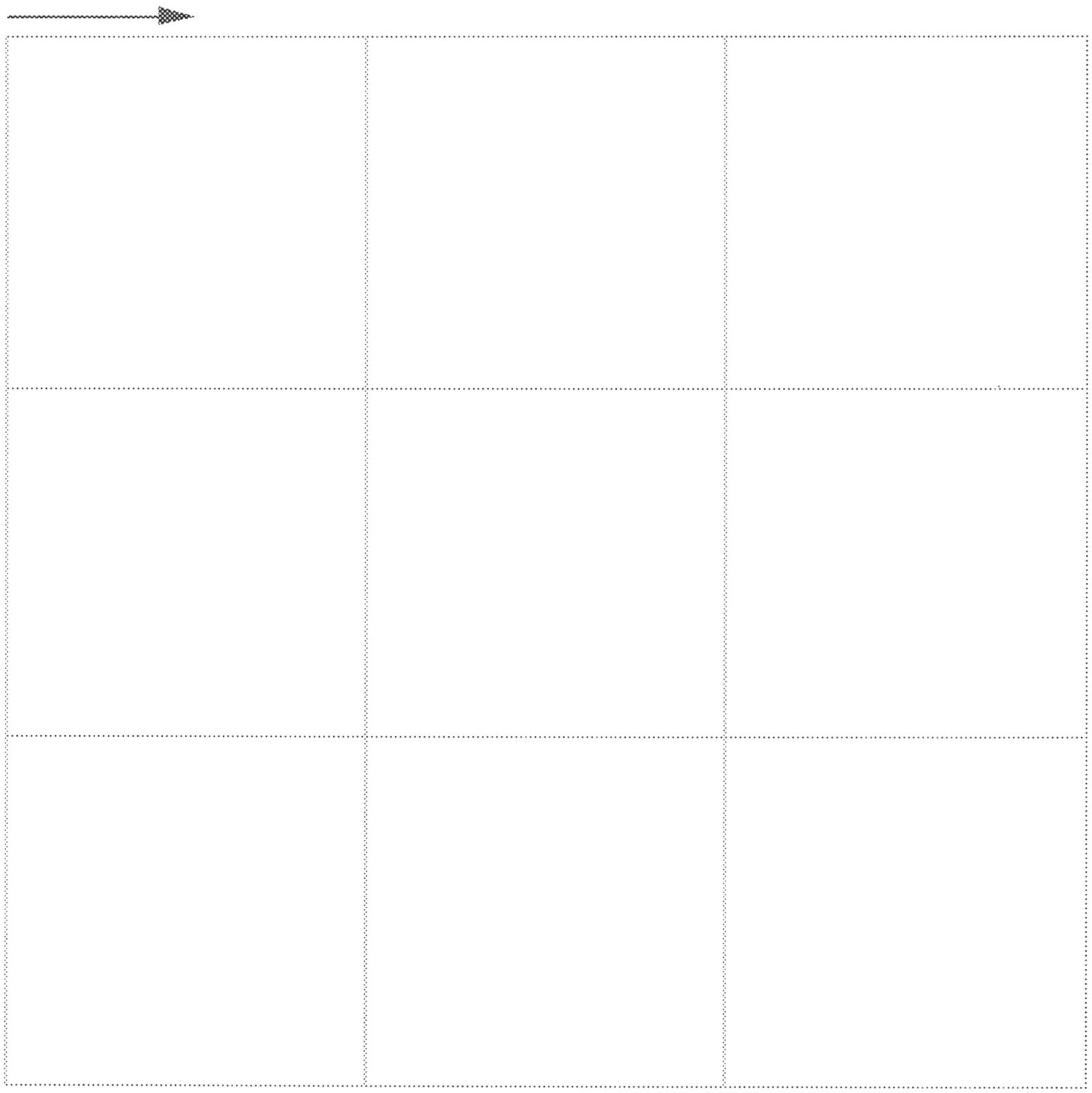

101 Seed Shapes

More Circles

- **Start with the circle.**

clock

Crystal ball

Bomb

- **Start with the top puff of circular shapes.**

Clouds

Lightning

Boom

103 *Seed Shapes*

©1993 Graphic Guides Inc.

Faces

- Begin with circle.

- Eyeballs are in the middle of the eye outline. Points show focus of attention.

- The mouth line shows emotion.

Happy

Sad

Confused

- **Details are like adjectives and adverbs.**

Really sad

Surprised

Hmmm?

Seed Shapes

More Faces

Nervous

Fried

Radiant

TIP *Try the practices then play off them: that's more fundamental than drawing "correctly."*

Angry

Frustrated

Sinister

CHAPTER 6

Star People

T HE SEVEN BASIC SHAPES AND THEIR IMPROVISATIONS ARE SUFFICIENT FOR MOST PURPOSES—ALONG WITH WRITTEN WORDS, OF COURSE. But the most basic shape of all for humans is the person. Learning to draw people turns out to be as simple as the other shapes.

There are many ways to draw simple people. Architects all have their favorite little people for illustrating their plans. This practice section introduces you to the star person. It can be drawn quickly, and has the advantage of being able to accept other elements easily—thus qualifying as an excellent "seed" shape.

Star Person Stroke Order

- The star person seed shape involves drawing a series of throw lines, each followed by a momentary hesitation to re-focus. This hesitation is built into the basic procedure and allows you to re-direct any of the individual throw lines, thereby opening the door to the variations on the following pages.

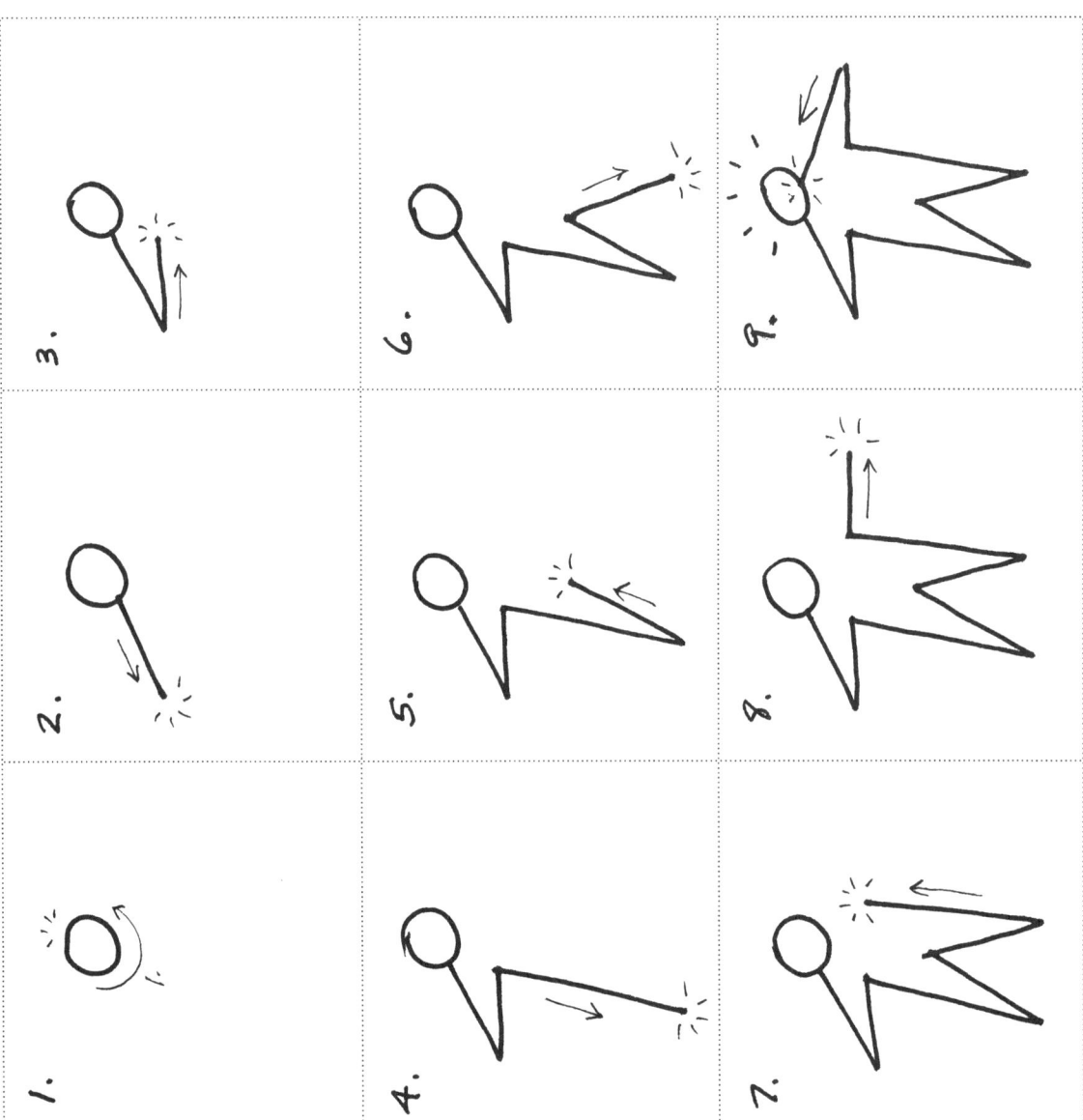

110 Star People

©1993 Graphic Guides Inc.

- Repeat the star person nine times in the spaces to the right.
- Play with the lengths and shapes of the arms and legs, and the head size until you love the little person you are drawing.
- Remember—Center, Focus, Draw.

TIP *Most important here is anchoring the throw lines and stroke order in your body—and keep your pen on the paper!*

Directing Attention

- Repeat each drawing three times.

Aim the first stroke high.

Wait til the last arm to aim high

Aim both arms high

112 *Star People*

add a "thumb bump" to make me point

Point me the other way

scratch my head with your first line

113 *Star People*

Hands and Feet

add little star hands

...or feet!

...or both.

make me reach... by gumming to the left on the tops

make me direct an orchestra

make me sad

115 Star People

©1993 Graphic Guides Inc.

Improvise!

add shading to stand me on the ground

or to jump

uh oh!

Star People

Give me star wings.

Add paraphernalia

or words

← THIS BIG →

117 Star People

©1993 Graphic Guides Inc.

Women and Men

add long hair –

and skirts –

or pants –

© 1993 Graphic Guides Inc.

Star People

Add a tie

or cowboy hat

or overalls

Star People

Expression

Make me talk

Make me think

Make me envision

I'm Angry
(Draw the arms first)

(I'm meditating)

I'm being polite

Star People

Combinations

Draw two of us —

add a contract —

or interaction arrows

122 *Star People*

©1993 Graphic Guides Inc.

draw something under my feet (don't draw me... just the line)

I'm riding a fast project

I'm on the train.

123 Star People

©1993 Graphic Guides Inc.

Combinations

vary size to get children

add heads in back for crowds

or in a circle for a team.

124   Star People

©1993 Graphic Guides Inc.

I'm presenting

I'm leading a group

I'm heading a table

Star People

The Sitting Person

Sit me down...by drawing my seat first

face me the other way

add an arm

126 *Star People*

Sit me on a crescent chair...it's simple and modern

Sit me the other way

Show my could by just drawing it

127 Star People

©1993 Graphic Guides Inc.

Meeting Combinations

Teacher Student

Negotiators

Small meeting

Training

Lecture

Celebration

CHAPTER 7

Putting
It All
Together

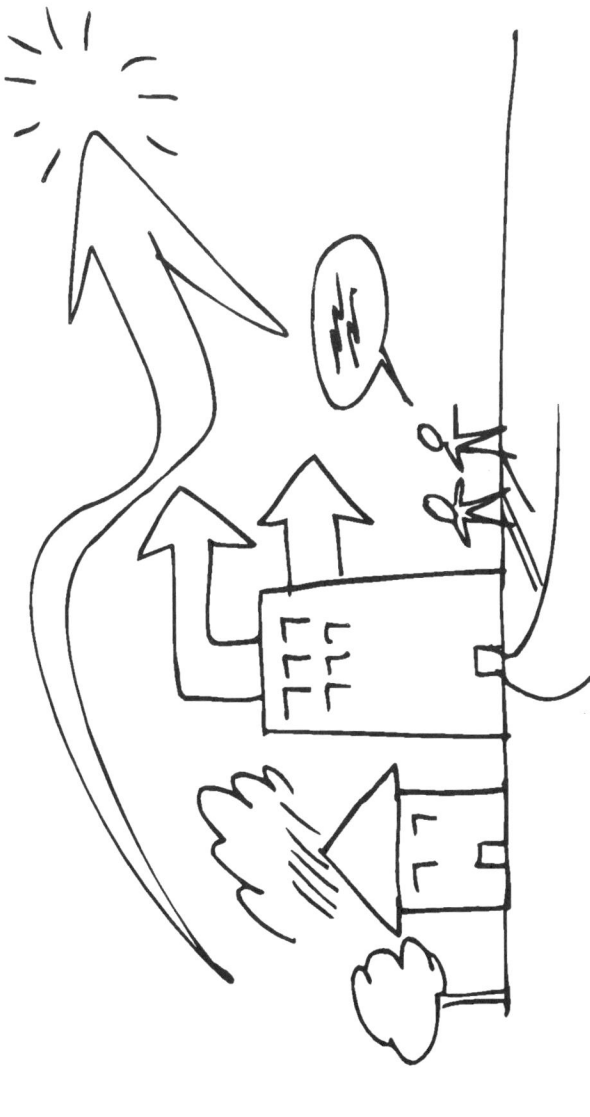

RAPHIC LANGUAGE COMES TO LIFE WHEN YOU COMBINE THE SEED SHAPES AND WORDS INTO GROUPS OF DRAWINGS WHICH REPRESENT "GRAPHIC SENTENCES."

In this chapter are some useful collections to practice with. Many more are possible—the secret to making graphic language your own is to create your own!

Meeting

1. Start with the heads. Arrange so they follow a gentle arc.
2. Draw the left person first.
3. Draw the front people next. Legs aren't necessary.
4. Finish with the right-hand person.
5. Draw the flip chart and standing person. Don't draw over the other figures—just lift your pen.
6. Throw shadow lines "away" from a central point.
7. Add aura lines, talk balloons, or whatever.

■ **Draw the pictures above in the boxes below. Have fun!**

 TIP *Draw a familiar object smaller, and it will seem further away.*

Putting It All Together

"U" Shape Training

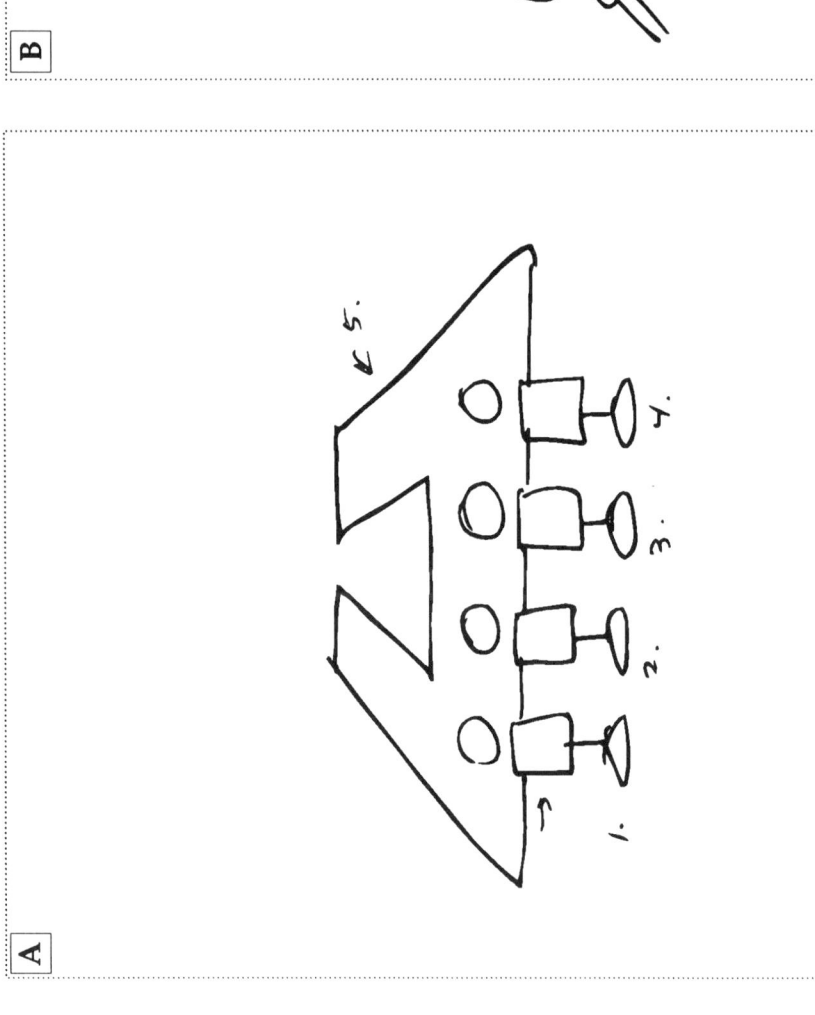

1. Draw the foreground figures first.
2. Draw the left-angle line then the horizon line, lifting the pen as you near a person.
3. Complete the table.
4. Add heads on the left and right.
5. Add bodies to the closest people.
6. Draw the person in front.
7. Add the chart.

■ **Draw the pictures above in the boxes below. Have fun!**

TIP *Draw lines converging to a point on a horizon line, and the viewer will see in perspective.*

Project

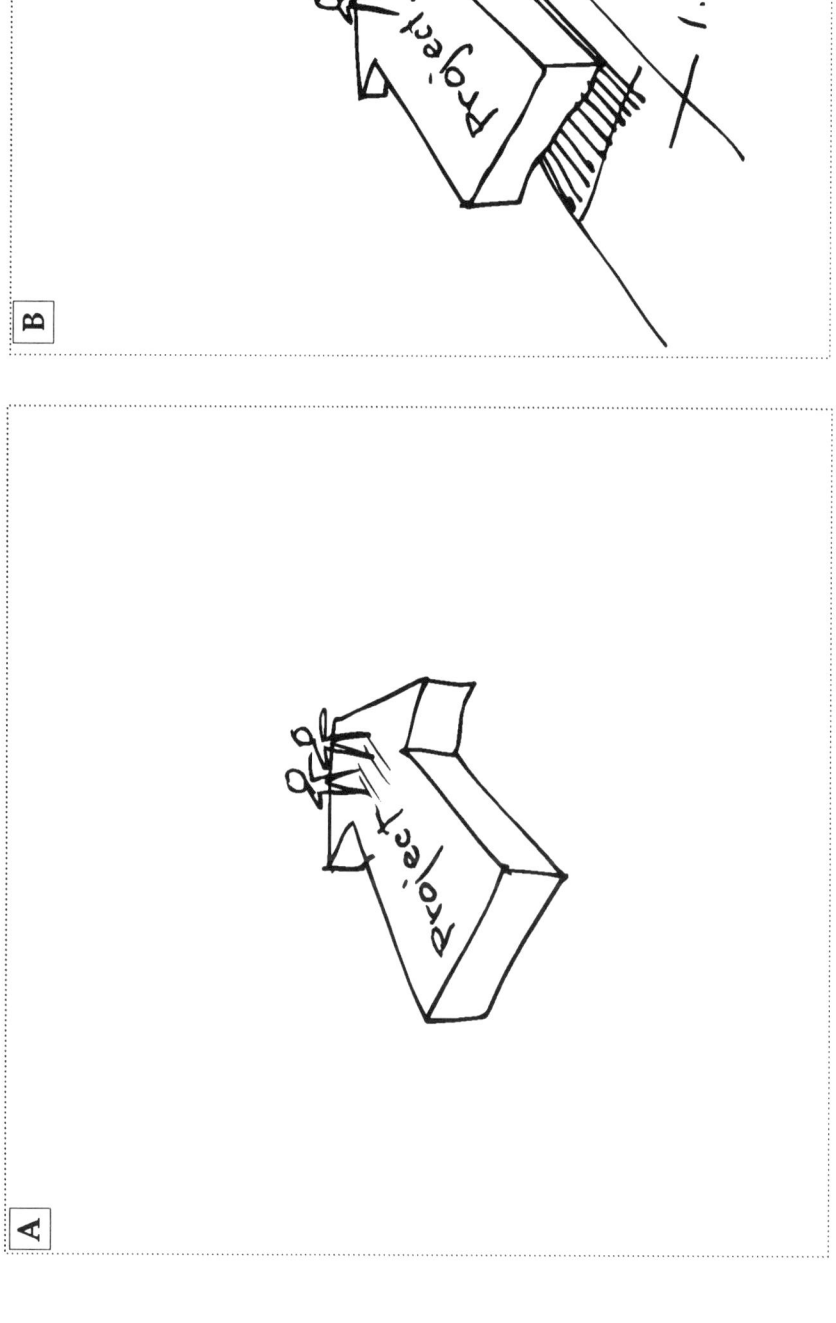

1. Draw the top arrow first.
2. Add drop lines and base lines.
3. Place star people.
4. Create the horizon.
5. Draw road lines.
6. Add shadows.
7. Write in information specific to your situation.

■ **Draw the pictures above in the boxes below. Have fun!**

TIP *Have graphics be faithful to the nature of the phenomena they're describing—formal projects with ruled lines, human resource projects with zig zagginess, or arcs and streaks.*

Putting It All Together 137

©1993 Graphic Guides Inc.

Cityscape

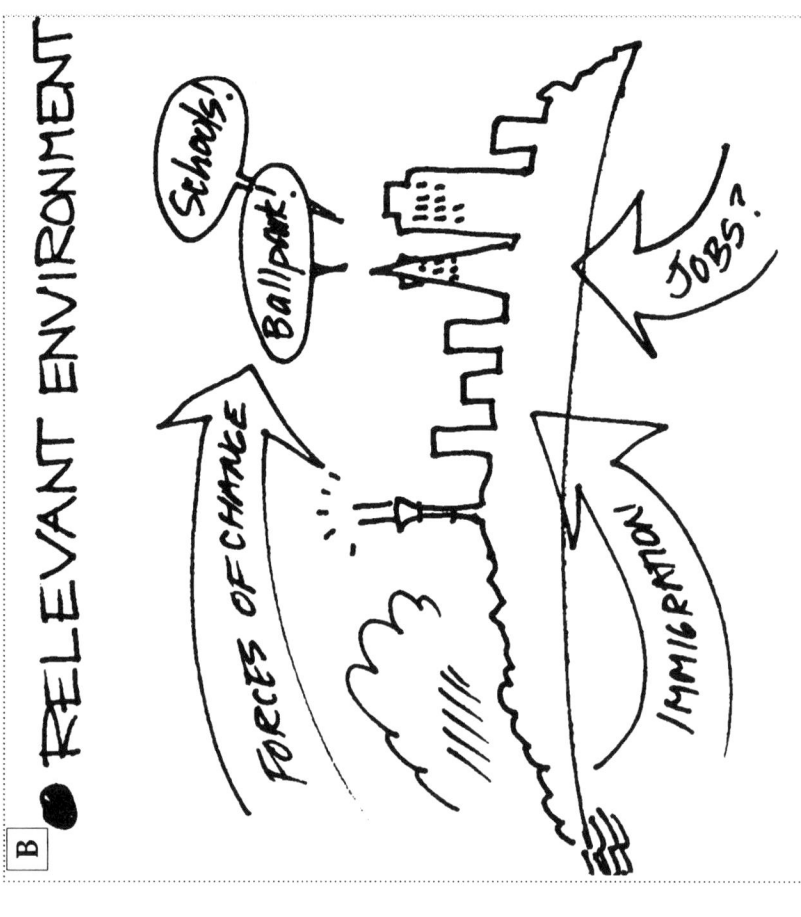

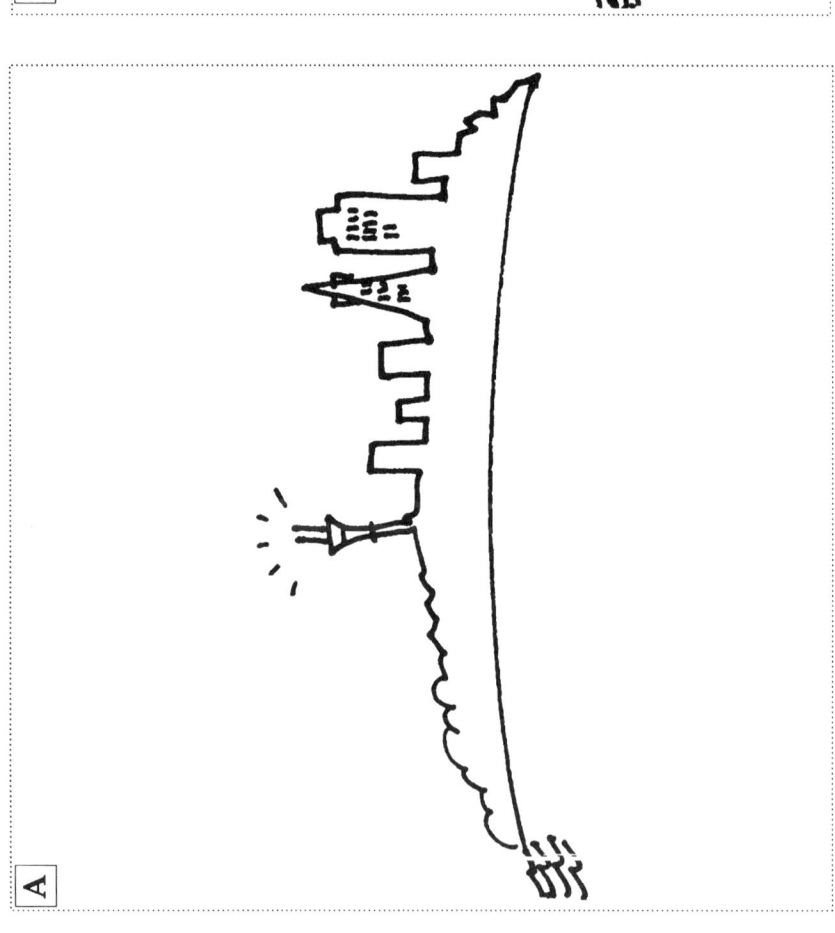

1. Draw the skyline combining pictographs into one line and include one or two well-known landmarks.

2. Add atmospheric elements specific to the situation.

3. Add a title so people can think of what they know and "project" in additional details.

- **Draw the pictures above in the boxes below. Have fun!**

TIP *For empowering, facilitating, and stimulating—silly ambiguous drawings suggest people more than exact ones.*

Natural Landscape

1. Begin with major features; mountains, river, shore.

2. Add features and shading. Text can be added to the ground or sky.

TIP *Distinguish between near and far objects by giving closer ones more detail.*

■ **Draw the pictures above in the boxes below. Have fun!**

TIP *Practice with these tools until you feel they are extensions of your arm expression.*

Thanks to Suzyn Benson, Suzanne Masica, Tomi Nagai-Rothe, Vera Resch, Jackie Sax, Thom Sibbet, Robert Pardini, and many in the Graphic Guides network who added suggestions to this second version.

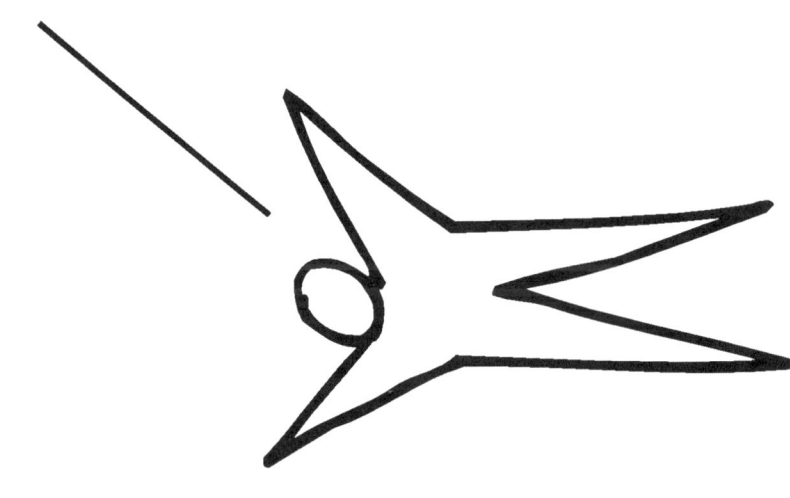